T0314738

G. H. Q.
(MONTREUIL-SUR-MER)

Haig – The Chief

G. H. Q.

(MONTREUIL-SUR-MER)

BY

"G. S. O."

WITH A MAP AND THIRTY-THREE ILLUSTRATIONS.

Incorporating the "GAME BOOK" of certain statistics appertaining to the period 8th August, 1918 to March 1919, compiled by Lieutenant Sir Travers Clarke, Quartermaster General (QMG).

UNIFORM

This edition published by Uniform, 2017
an imprint of Unicorn Publishing Group

Unicorn Publishing Group
101 Wardour Street
London W1F 0UG
www.unicornpublishing.org

Beaumont Fox, 37 St.James's Place, London SW1A 1NS
02076290981
www.sirfrankfox.com

2nd Edition, First Published by Philip Allan & Co.,
Quality Court, Chancery Lane, W.C. 1920

ISBN 978-1-910500-83-5

Printed and bound in UK

The image on the front cover *Haig – The Chief,* is by John C. Johansen and
is reproduced by kind permission of his Grandson, Lord Astor of Hever.

CONTENTS

LIST OF ILLUSTRATIONS

FOREWORD

by Doctor Charles Goodson-Wickes,
Great Grandson and Literary Executor of Sir Frank Fox

Sir Frank Fox was a journalist, author, soldier and campaigner.
Having been attached to the Belgian Army as War Correspondent for the Morning Post at the time of the German Invasion in 1914, he wrote a unique account of the atrocities visited upon the civilian population. Some of these eye witness accounts were initially not believed by the Belgian and British authorities in Brussels.

However those events were the stimulus for his seeking a combatant role in the Great War. He was commissioned (aged 41) into the British Army in December 1914 and was posted to France.

In the Battle of the Somme he was twice wounded. After the second occasion he was hospitalised for a year in England and then worked for MI7. Fretting at being away from the action, he pulled strings to be sent back to France.

He was posted to Montreuil-sur-Mer to join Haig's Staff at GHQ. He must have cut a curious figure on crutches having lost part of his right foot, and having a withered left arm. His profound deafness cannot have added to added to the overall impression.

His work in the QMG's Directorate in the final offensive against the German Army resulted in his being awarded the OBE (Military) He was also Mentioned in Despatches.
This book is another unique contemporary account, and was originally published under the pseudonym "GSO". It received much critical acclaim.

It is republished here with the "Game Book" as an Appendix. This statistical record was privately published for King George V and only 6 copies were made.

Dr. Charles Goodson-Wickes
NOVEMBER 2015

PREFACE

That fantastic life at G.H.Q., so greatly detached from the normal—the life of the men whose words had power to send Armies into and out of action, to give this Division rest and surcease from the agony of the struggle, to assign to that Division the stress of a new effort; the men into whose hands the nation poured millions without stint and at whose call the whole world moved to spin or dig or forge—will it be of interest now to recall some of its memories, to attempt an intimate picture of its routine?

Fantastic the life was truly. One man of imagination, who had done his work in the line so well as to win a reputation for great courage and administrative ability, and had carried through with a quiet skill and a simple dutifulness the responsibilities of the "small family" of a regiment, found, when he was transferred to G.H.Q., that the sense of responsibility was too great for his temperament. He was not a very important cog of the machine. But the feeling that the motion which his hand started set going so great a series of actions got on his nerves to the extent that he could neither sleep nor eat with comfort, nor decide the simplest matter without torturing doubt as to whether it were right or wrong. He "moved on" within a few days.

Fortunately that sense of vision was rare. The average man was content to "carry on" with his task with what good judgment Heaven gave him, deciding as the established routine, or the commonsense shift of a new emergency, dictated.

But looking back, reflecting on all the woeful results that might have sprung from a careless blunder, from too great haste, from too deliberate hesitation, from over fear or over confidence, it is to be seen how fantastic, how abnormal was the life centred in that little walled town of Montreuil, the focus of a spider's web of wires, at one end of which were the soldiers in their trenches, at the other the workers of the world at their benches. Yet we ate, drank, slept, played a little and talked, very much as if we were workers in some commercial house, directing coffee from a plantation to a warehouse and then to a breakfast table, instead of dealing in blood and tears, drawing without stint on human life and human hope so that the idea of Right and Liberty might be saved in the world.

It is well that Imagination went to sleep, or was lacking. For so the work could be done and the war directed to its safe conclusion. But a record of the life we lived seems now, in retrospect, almost indecorous. It is as if we should not have munched food, talked trivialities, while before our eyes and under our hands was played out the greatest tragedy Man has known; as if it would have been more fitting if we had gone from uneasy couches, tightlipped and anxious, to our desks, haunted always by a sense of doom.

It was not like that. And, such as it was, I attempt to record it—a serious enough life in any sense of the word, monkish in its denial of some pleasures, rigid in discipline, exacting in work, but neither austere nor anxious—such a life as studious boys might live in a Public School, if there can be imagined a Public School in which sport was reduced to the minimum essential to keep one fit for hard "swotting." But a life with some relaxations, and some pleasures, cheerful, actually lighthearted.

Questions of the conduct of the war must obtrude somewhat in this book, but it will be only in so much as they are a necessary background to the story of the life of G.H.Q.—of G.H.Q. in its later phase when it had moved from St. Omer to Montreuil and had become what it was in the final result, a capable Board of Directors of as glorious a company of soldiers as the world has known. There will be no attempt at a history of the war, no battle pictures, which are usually vain efforts to measure the immeasurable. Yet it is hoped that the reader will get from it some idea of the character and the complexities of the struggle.

Already fogs of controversy are obscuring many of the facts of the war. There is a controversy whether the first Commander-in-Chief should have been recalled when he was; about the merits of the second Commander-in-Chief; about the "unity of command" decision; about the relative merits of a strategy which would concentrate everything for a supreme effort in France and a strategy which would seek a "back door" to the German citadel; about the actual cause and duration of the shell shortage. In accordance with our British custom we are mostly taking sides, following some leader and putting our faith in his views, and all his views, implicitly. Thus are formed parties. I claim with honesty, and perhaps with correctness, not to belong to any of the parties. I have set down these observations on G.H.Q. without a thought of whether they may support this view or that view on the conduct of the war.

THE AUTHOR.

THE BOULOGNE GATE

12

G.H.Q.

CHAPTER I.

BEFORE G.H.Q. WENT TO MONTREUIL.

The first stages of the War—"Trench War," a good German invention—The Battle of Eyes—Waiting for the Big Push—The Loos disappointment—Moving G.H.Q. to Montreuil.

IT was the task of General Headquarters to try to see the War as a whole, to obtain a knowledge not only of the strictly military situation but, to an extent, also of the moral and the political situation of the enemy and of our own forces. In the later stages of the campaign that task was being done, *pace* all the critics, with an efficiency that was wonderful, seeing that before the Great War the British nation did not allow its Army any chance at all of war practice on a big scale. Our Generals, whatever skill they might have won in studying the theory of war, had had no opportunity to practise big movements. They were very much in the position of men trained in the running of a small provincial store who were asked suddenly to undertake the conduct of one of the mammoth "universal providers."

It is of G.H.Q. in the later stages of the war that I write, not G.H.Q. of the earlier stages, when our Army was finding its feet. But a slight generalisation regarding those earlier stages is necessary to an understanding of the subsequent growth of the Army organisation and of its Board of Directors at G.H.Q.

The small Army which crossed to France in 1914 was organised as an Expeditionary Force for a war of movement. It did gallant work in the first phase, as all have admitted. When the war of movement stopped and the struggle settled down to the War of the Trenches, though that gave a good opportunity of recruiting, it brought up an entirely new set of problems, for which our organisation had made no provision at all and in which British natural gifts did not have the best chance of display. Indeed our training system at home refused in 1914-15 to "recognise" Trench War. The New Armies were trained on the same lines as the old Regular Army, but of course more hurriedly, more intensively, less efficiently. They learned Trench Warfare—an almost entirely different game—when they got out to the Front. A reversal of the process—to have taught the much simpler Trench Warfare in the home camps and left the teaching of movement warfare to training intervals in France was an obviously more economical system, and it was that adopted at a later stage.

When a considered history of the war comes to be written, probably it will give to the German High Command high praise for this period of "Trench War." It was the one conspicuously good invention of the enemy. It enabled him almost completely to stop the war in the one theatre where he had to meet troops superior to his own, whilst his forces ranged round Europe winning cheap victories and finally (though too late as it proved) vanquishing opposition elsewhere. There is no doubt that the Trench War device baffled our side for a time. I like the story of Marshal Joffre explaining the position to an American war correspondent and adding:

"You see there is nothing to be done."

"No. I suppose nobody could do anything?"

"Nobody."

"Not even Napoleon?"

But Marshal Joffre paused at that, and after a moment's reflection said:

"Yes, I suppose Napoleon could do something."

Finally the "something" came in the shape of the "Tank."

When Field Marshal Earl Haig took over the chief command he adopted the system of frequent "raids" to give to the Trench War some of the character of moving war, and that proved a highly useful step. Still, this Trench War was not of the genius of our people; and it was very dull. If I were seeking the fit adjective which could be applied to it in its superlative it would certainly not be "exciting" nor yet "dangerous." The life was exciting and it was dangerous—a little. It was, however, neither very exciting nor very dangerous. But it was very, very curious. Trench war had its moments, its hours of high emotion, of intense excitement, of crowding dangers. Its routine—on the Western front—was laborious, almost to the point of tediousness, demanding a sober and constant carefulness in detail, and—provided you watched the minutes and the winds, the twigs and the sky, had eyes, ears, and nerves always on the alert—it was reasonably safe.

Trench War exciting? No; you could not allow it to be. The moments were rare (to the majority of officers they never came) when the call was for a gallant shout and a forward rush in which leadership took its most obvious and its easiest form. The hours were always when, with cool, suspicious, deducting mind, you were watching a sector, awaiting the enemy's raiding attack or directing your own. Stalking and being stalked, it was interesting, absorbing, but you could not allow it to be exciting, or you would not do your work properly. War was robbed, in that phase of the struggle, of most of its fascinations by the spectacled Germans who had spent the previous half-century in the counting house, the laboratory, and the cellar, preparing to destroy the humanities of civilisation. Trench War was a grubbing kind of business.

Dangerous? Naturally, to an extent. But not nearly so dangerous as one might judge from the lurid accounts of imaginative writers. It had its hours of peril, of horror. But it was not all the time dangerous. For six days out of seven, on an average, a soldier, if he observed the strictest caution, was "following a dangerous trade," nothing more. On the seventh day—I speak in averages—he had his risk about doubled. On very rare occasions he had to take the risk of a fireman who goes into a blazing house to rescue a child, or a policeman who stops a madly bolting horse. Ordinarily one had to be careful "to watch the traffic;" that was all. If you wished to take a long lingering look at the enemy's trench you used a periscope. For a brief glance (to get a wide field of view) you looked over the parapet. There were differing estimates of the length of time it was safe to show your head over the parapet. Some said five seconds, others twenty-five.

"The German is slow in the up-take," remarked the officer who insisted that twenty-five seconds was quite a safe time to look over the parapet.

Behind the parapet it was almost as safe—and on dry days as pleasant—as on a marine parade. A solid fortification of sandbags, proof against any blow except that of a big high-explosive shell, enclosed on each side a walk, drained, paved, lined with dug-outs, in places adorned with little flower beds. I write, of course, of the Trench War in its "settled" stage—not of those grim struggles around Ypres in the Autumn of 1914.

Not exciting, not as dangerous as one would imagine, the Trench War was more curious, more "uncanny," than it is possible to describe. Try to imagine the huge ditch, some 300 miles long, from the North Sea to the Swiss lakes, which was our trench, facing another ditch which was their trench, all lined with Eyes, thousands, millions of Eyes. All day, all night, these Eyes stare and stare. At night the hands serving them break up the dark with star shells, and the brains behind them welcome the day, only because it makes the scrutiny of Death more easy. On the front edge of each ditch the Eyes are thick in line, farther back, in every possible post of observation, are groups of Eyes, and Eyes soar up into the air now and again to stare into the secrets concealed on the other side. There are Eyes of infantry, Eyes of artillery, Eyes of airmen. The scrutiny never pauses for an instant. Let an Eye blink a moment and it may mean catastrophe, a stealthy rush on a trench or a flood of poisoning gas. The great dark gutter stretching across Belgium and France was fringed with staring Eyes; and every Eye had to record its message to G.H.Q.

Carefulness, tedious, monotonous carefulness, absolute punctuality, and grave attention to every detail—these were the warrior qualities in the Trench War period. The minutes had to be watched, the grass watched lest you trod down a path and gave away some secret to the Eyes yonder. All the minute details of life were hedged in with precautions and penalties.

This tedious Trench War was not the game for British blood, though on the whole it was done well, especially after Loos when the raiding policy was instituted. But it was tedious; and very clearly it was impossible to win while it lasted. For victory the Germans had to be turned out of those trenches. So, during the tedium of the Trench War we would comfort ourselves with the thought that very soon the Big Push must come. Often the most definite news came that it was fixed for the next month. This very definite news was usually traced back to some signaller who had overheard something on the telephone. Perhaps Divisional H.Q. had a Member of Parliament (doing a "Cook's tour" of the Front) to dinner and peremptory messages were going down to the Coast asking for lobsters to be sent up. Now a guileless signaller would never imagine that Generals and the like were interested in lobster. If he thought of their diet at all he probably imagined they lived on trench maps—of which the consumption was certainly huge. Thus the signaller, hearing strange peremptory messages about lobsters, might conclude that this was some very secret code, and, the Big Push being in all our thoughts, that it would have reference to that most certainly. But for many months it was not the Big Push; it was only the lobster, which was the standard of gaiety and dissipation at a Mess Dinner.

BEFORE G.H.Q. WENT TO MONTREUIL.

At the time of the Loos attack it did really seem that the Big Push had come. But we were disappointed. Perhaps at the Front we were as impatient at the result as the people at home, but we could soothe our impatience with the thought of the greatness of the technical difficulties of arranging an advance with a battle-line hundreds of miles in length, all entrenched (difficulties which did not occur to those gentlemen who wrote weekly expert articles, to show how it should be done). It was clear that if we could push forward a little at certain vital points, a rich reward would be reaped. We knew that what would seem the obvious thing—to press along the whole line and break through in the weak parts—would have only landed us in a number of advanced salients which would be hard, or impossible, to defend when they came under enfilade fire. There were scores of places in which the German would willingly have let us through; to destroy the advanced party afterwards. We had to aim to push in wedges at our own selected points where the salient thus formed could be defended and could seriously threaten a German line of communication. It was not easy, for the number of those points was limited and the German knew them all.

Loos showed very plainly what we were "up against." There was a long pause for further preparation, a pause which seemed unendurably long at the time when the French were taking such a hammering at Verdun and we were going on with tedious Trench War and still more tedious preparations behind the lines.

Criticism of the British military effort at this stage of the war was fairly general and sometimes very hostile. Some assumed that we had tried our last blow at Loos and that we would never do more than hold a trench sector until the French could finish the war. At Home there were critics who argued that the British military effort would have been more wisely directed if, in the first stage of the war, the British Expeditionary Force had been kept at home and used as the nucleus for training a great continental army, ignoring the pressing circumstances of August, 1914.

Undoubtedly in that way a great British Army could have been far more quickly raised. Undoubtedly, too, the task of forming the new British Army was very seriously handicapped by the draining away to France of practically all the fully-trained men of military age in Great Britain. But with a choice of two courses Great Britain took the more daring and the more generous one; and that in human affairs is generally the better one. The material help which the Five Divisions of the British Army gave to the French was not negligible. The moral help was much greater. The lack of those Divisions might have lost Paris to the French and left the Germans in control of all France north and east of the Seine; and that event might have ended the war—it would certainly have prejudiced seriously the French recovery.

The risk taken by Great Britain in stripping her own territory of its only efficient army was not inconsiderable. Direct attack by Germany was seriously feared then. A bolder German naval policy, indeed, might have secured an invasion of England. Plans were drawn up in England at one time on the supposition of a German descent on our coasts being successful in its first stages, and it was proposed to meet this by converting a wide coastal section of England into a desert.

Criticism was to be silenced in time, for presently we were to open that giant battle which was not to finish until November, 1918, and which was then to finish with the British Army the most important force in the Field.

G.H.Q. moved to Montreuil on March 31st, 1916. On the same date, it may be said, the British Army in France came to man's estate. It had been up to this an "auxiliary army" holding a small section of the front, and a "training army" getting ready to take over—as ultimately it did take over—the main burden of the war; for, counting its captures of prisoners and guns from August, 1918, to November 11th, 1918, the British Army's share in the final victory was almost equal to that of the French, American and Belgian forces combined.

G.H.Q. came to Montreuil because St. Omer, the old G.H.Q. town, was no longer suitable as the centre for the vast operations pending. It had served well enough when we formed the left wing of the French battle line. Now we were to be the spear-head of the thrust against Germany.

Look back upon the little British Army of at first four and then five Divisions, which in 1914 took rank alongside the French by Mons, and fell back fighting until the rally of the Marne; and then upon the Army of 1916 of ten times the strength, which was directed from Montreuil. The growth shows as marvellous, and especially so to those who understand how an army in the field is comparable to an iceberg at sea, of which the greater part is unseen. For every rifleman in the trenches and gunner in the gun-pits there are at least three other people working to keep him supplied with food, clothing, ammunition, and on communications. So an Army's growth demands a growth behind the line three times as great as that in the line. And this growth is not merely a matter of the multiplication of riflemen and gunners and auxiliaries, a heaping up of men. It must be an organic growth to be effective at all; an adding one by one of highly complex and yet homogeneous units.

A "Division" is the integral unit of any Army, and a Division must have in the field its infantry battalions, cavalry or cyclist companies, field batteries, signallers (with "wireless," telephone and telegraph service), engineers, transport and supply services, medical and ambulance services. All told, it numbered about 17,000 officers and men at the close of the war, but in 1914 the strength of a Division was nearer to 20,000. And this body of 20,000 was not a mob, nor a crowd, nor yet even a simple organization such as a band of factory employees. It was a nation in microcosm, its constituent numbers covering almost the whole of the activities of life. It had to be organised to fight, to keep up communications, to manufacture and repair, to feed itself and its horses, to keep good health conditions in its camps and to succour its sick and wounded. Besides fighting men it had doctors, vets., sanitary engineers, mechanics of all kinds, chemists, electricians. Behind the line the Division's supports, its munition and clothing factories, its food providers, had to be organised just as carefully.

Nothing can be made without making mistakes, and in the carrying out of this giant task of making the Army of the British Empire there were many mistakes of detail. It is in the nature of the human mind to see such mistakes in high relief, as the human eye sees small patches of stone stand out from a vast field of snow. But, making the worst that can be made of the mistakes, if they are seen in proper perspective they cannot blur the dazzling brilliance of a marvellous achievement.

Most of the mistakes, moreover, were direct consequences of that innocence of warlike intention and that passion for human right and liberty which was common to Great Britain as to the rest of Western Europe, and on which, clearly, the German Powers had counted as sufficient to paralyse effective resistance to their deliberate and designed preparation. Hindering those good qualities of peacefulness proved to be, but not paralysing. After all, the task was done. That most dangerous first rush of German militarism was stayed. The powerful beast was kept within bounds whilst weapons were forged for his destruction. In vain were all his efforts, backed by the skill of half a century of preparation and Spartan discipline.

G. H. Q. (MONTREUIL-SUR-MER)

Montreuil was chosen as G.H.Q. for a wide variety of reasons. It was on a main road from London to Paris—the two chief centres of the campaign—though not on a main railway line, which would have been an inconvenience. It was not an industrial town and so avoided the complications alike of noise and of a possibly troublesome civil population. It was from a telephone and motor transit point of view in a very central situation to serve the needs of a Force which was based on Dunkirk, Calais, Boulogne, Dieppe, and Havre, and had its front stretching from the Somme to beyond the Belgian frontier.

A great general, asked to define in a phrase what was wanted for a Headquarters, said "A central remoteness." It was urged that this seemed an oxymoron. "Well then, if you like, a remote centrality." The finality of that allowed of no further argument. Montreuil provided both a central position and a position remote from the disturbances and distractions of traffic, of a large population, of gay social interests. The great Ecole Militaire offered accommodation for the chief offices. There was sufficient billeting accommodation in the town houses and the neighbouring chateaux.

BEFORE G.H.Q. WENT TO MONTREUIL.

THE 'CAVÉE' SAINT FIRMIN

G. H. Q. (MONTREUIL-SUR-MER)

G.H.Q. of course was never a great camp. Its total military population was never more than 5,000, including those G.H.Q. troops who were needed for guards and who were drawn first from the Artists' Rifles, then from the Honourable Artillery Company, then from the Newfoundland Regiment, and finally from the Guernsey Regiment. Accommodation at Montreuil was reinforced somewhat by hutments in 1917-18, but on the whole the town was big enough for its purpose.

CHAPTER II.

MONTREUIL AND THE MONTREUILLOIS.

How the Montreuillois once learned to hate the English— Early history of the famous town—Its link with the early Roman-British Empire—A border town in the Anglo- French Wars—When G.H.Q. was bombed.

MILITARY convenience alone dictated the choice of Montreuil as the site of the General Headquarters of the British Expeditionary Force in France as soon as that Force reached to such a strength as to take its full share in the campaign. But the choice might well have been influenced by a sentimental desire to make this town, which was so intimately associated with the old enmity between England and France, the centre of the Great Reconciliation. Montreuil and the Montreuillois for many centuries cordially hated England, and not without good reason. In April, 1369, they chased the English from the town with hoots of *"A la queue, à la queue les Anglais."* After 550 years, in April, 1919, they saw the British G.H.Q. leave Montreuil with what different feelings!

Very curious is the way in which Montreuil has been linked up with Anglo-French history. In the days of the Roman occupation of Gaul the Roman Empire had a naval station close to, or actually on, the great fortress rock which guarded the mouth of the Canche and which was then a peninsula jutting out into the sea. This station, no doubt, Julius Cæsar used in his expedition against Britain. Later Carausius, a Roman Briton, revolted against the Roman Empire and, by winning the command of the Channel with his Fleet, maintained for a time an independent Britain. He assumed the state of Cæsar and founded a Roman-British Empire. The *Classis Britannica* of the Roman Empire had had its chief station at or near Montreuil. With the revolt of Carausius there was no longer a "British Fleet" of the Roman Empire, and the *Classis Samarica* (the Fleet of the Somme) was organised to hold the coasts of Gaul for the Roman Power against the British rebel, Carausius. This Fleet of the Somme had a station on the Canche, at or near Montreuil. Doubtless in those very early years of the Christian era there was many a naval action between the British sea forces and those of the Romans stationed on the Canche.

Of any actual Roman buildings on the hill of Montreuil there exists to-day no trace. But it may be accepted as certain that the Gauls had fortified this great hill at the mouth of the Canche and that the Roman Conquerors did not neglect its strategical advantages. It is well within the bounds of the historic imagination to picture Carausius, the man who first taught England that her fate depended on the holding of the Narrow Seas, looking with vain hostility on a well-fortified Roman naval station at Montreuil which often sent harassing expeditions against his coast. In later years of Anglo-French enmity Montreuil was Montreuil-sur-mer only in name, for the sea had retreated ten miles, and Etaples was the port at the mouth of the Canche; but in the Roman days and for some centuries after, Montreuil was a good harbour for trade or for war.

When the barbarian invasions overwhelmed the Roman Empire, Montreuil disappeared from history until the Seventh Century, when the monk St. Saulve (subsequently Bishop of Amiens) built a monastery on the great hill. From this monastery, without much doubt, the name of Montreuil comes; for in all old French manuscripts it is spelt "Monsereul," which is an easy step from "Monasteriolum," "the place of the monastery." In St. Saulve's day Montreuil appears to have been a bold promontory at the edge of the sea, with the River Canche running close to its base and a thriving village at its foot. According to some accounts, St. Saulve's first monastery was built on the ruins of an earlier castle; if so it would probably have been a castle of Roman origin.

Montreuil became a famous shrine, and reports came from it of many miracles. The Saints Omer, Riquier, Bertin and Josse, whose names are kept on record in St. Omer and other neighbouring towns and villages, were monks of the Montreuil monastery. There is a Forest of Josse just near Montreuil, and I regret to say that some American officers were persuaded to believe that it got its name from being the site of a Chinese Labour Joss-house, to the lessening of the glory of St. Josse.

With the ravages of the pirate Northmen another period of darkness falls upon the town of Montreuil until the 9th century, when the famous Count Hildgood (that is to say "hold-good," a stubborn man in the fight) resolved to make head against the Northmen, and in defence of his county of Ponthieu built on Montreuil Hill a strong fortress. Traces of this fortress still exist in the town. The Hotel de France (which was a meeting place for officers of G.H.Q. when a dinner away from Mess formalities was desired) stands on part of the site of "Hold-good's" fortress.

Count Hildgood was something of a statesman as well as a soldier, and encouraged a civilian population to collect at the foot of his fortress, and used the glory of St. Saulve's monastery to attract to the place other religious communities from Brittany and elsewhere. Montreuil became thus a famous strong-point. It developed on the familiar lines of a mediæval city with its well-established local rights, those of "the peers of the peerage of Montreuil." The ravages of the Northmen in the surrounding country continued, but Montreuil was too strong for them and grew into a city of refuge, giving hospitality to many religious refugee communities even from as far away as Brittany.

It remained without dispute a part of the county of Ponthieu until 939, when, as related by the monkish historian Richer, it was coveted by the Count of Flanders and captured through the treachery of the governor, Robert le Chepier. (One of the towers of the existing fortifications still bears his name). The children of the Count of Ponthieu were taken captives and sent to the English Court to be held as prisoners—giving rise to one of the first of the many grudges that the good Montreuillois had against England. The Count of Ponthieu appealed for help to the then Duke of Normandy (William of the Long Sword). The help was given, Montreuil was wrested from the Flemings, and handed back to the Count of Ponthieu according to some accounts, held by the Normans according to other accounts, which have a greater air of reasonableness, for the Normans were good at taking and slow at giving back.

G. H. Q. (MONTREUIL-SUR-MER)

OUTSIDE THE RAMPARTS

MONTREUIL AND THE MONTREUILLOIS.

But all disputes as to the possession of Montreuil between the Counts of Ponthieu and Flanders and the Duke of Normandy were settled by the King of France, Hugo Capet, who made the town part of the Royal Domain of France and built a great fortified château by the side of the old citadel. A part of this château still remains, "the Tower of Queen Bertha," so-called from the unhappy fate of Bertha, Queen of Philip I. of France. She was the daughter of the Count Florent I. of Holland, and had borne Philip three children when he became enamoured of the wife of the Count of Anjou and shut his own wife up to die in Montreuil. To quote the old chronicle: "Il la mist en prison en un fort chastel qui a nom Monstereul-sur-la-mer." The poor lady seems to have been most harshly treated, and was left dependent on the charity of the townsfolk for her food. The children of Montreuil recall the story to this day when begging for money for the churches with the cry "Give, give, to your Queen."

By this time the Norman Conquest had given England a place in European politics. The 13th Century brought Montreuil under the English Crown. Jeanne, Countess of Ponthieu and Montreuil, had married the King of Castille and Leon. Their daughter Eleonora of Castille married Edward I., King of England, and part of her dowry was Montreuil. Edward I. came over in 1279 to take over his new possession, and promised the Montreuillois to safeguard all their local rights and privileges. But the good folk of the town did not like the English of that day, and disputes were constant. They rejoiced when war broke out between France and England (a war in which the French had the Scots as allies and the English the Flemings); for the King of France exempted Montreuil from her feudal duty to the English King.

That war was stopped by the intervention of Pope Boniface, and a Peace Conference assembled at Montreuil. One of the peace conditions was that the Prince of Wales should marry the daughter of the King of France, and this marriage was celebrated with great magnificence at Boulogne, the young princess passing through Montreuil to the wedding. She received as her pin-money from her husband the revenues of Ponthieu and Montreuil.

But that marriage did not make for peace. On the contrary its fruits were a new series of wars interrupted by an occasional truce or brief peace. Crécy and Agincourt were both fought almost in sight of Montreuil. The district round was ravaged again and again by the English forces, and several times the town itself was besieged in vain.

G. H. Q. (MONTREUIL-SUR-MER)

After Crécy, Edward tried to take it and failed. An incident of one of the peace treaties was the visit of Chaucer, the poet, to Montreuil as an English plenipotentiary. An incident of one of the wars was the passage through Montreuil of the funeral procession of King Henry V.

So through the years Montreuil was in the very heart of the struggle between English and French. It was in a manner the border town between the territory in France which was admitted to be English, and the disputed territory. Thus it learned a deep hatred of the English. Often as a condition of peace it was handed over to English domination; never was it content with that destiny. Finally, the ambition of the English Kings to add France to their realms—an ambition which was as bad for England as it was for France—was definitely frustrated. Montreuil, passionately French in spirit, "the most faithful town in all Picardy," as Henry of Navarre called it, was no more to be vexed either by English governors or English marauders.

But Montreuil cherished its dislike of the English, and probably had never been so happy for centuries as when in 1804 it was the headquarters of the left wing of Napoleon's Army for the invasion of England. General Ney was the officer in command at Montreuil, and his brilliant receptions brought back to the town some of its Middle Ages pomp. It was from Montreuil that in 1804 General Ney addressed to Napoleon a memorial begging him to take the Imperial Crown for the sake of France. Napoleon himself visited Montreuil more than once, and a house in which he slept is still shown in the Place Verte.

Little or nothing of this was in the minds of our Staff in deciding upon Montreuil as a site for G.H.Q. It was convenient (as its choice in old times for Peace Conferences between England and France clearly shows) to London and to Paris. It was off any main traffic route, and promised quiet for telephone services. The feelings of the inhabitants were presumed to be friendly, and the presumption was justified, though curiously enough there was in 1918 a slight revival of the old anti-English feelings, and I even heard whispered again "*à la queue les Anglais.*" It all arose from what must be admitted to have been rather an undignified incident.

There used to be a fable—no one was fonder of giving it circulation than the Red Tabs—that there was a mutual agreement between the Germans and ourselves that G.H.Q. on both sides was to be spared from air raids.

"The arrangement is a classic instance of our stupidity," the Red

MONTREUIL AND THE MONTREUILLOIS.

Tab humorist would remark, "for the German scores both ways."

"How is that?"

"Well, his Staff is spared, which is valuable to him. And our Staff is spared, which is also valuable to him."

Staff officers, B.E.F., could afford to pass on gibes like that in 1917-18 when British Staff work was the model which the new American armies set themselves to imitate.

But as a matter of fact in the summer of 1918 G.H.Q. was bombed pretty regularly by the enemy. Those who lived there had unhappy proof of that. There were several deaths from bombs in and near the town. After the first bombing attacks orders were issued that no soldier, except sentries and officers on night duty, was to be allowed to sleep in Montreuil. The whole garrison was to go into the woods at night, or to take refuge in the deep dug-outs which were tunnelled under the city. Hardly a night passed without a bombing raid, until the tide of battle turned and the German bomber had neither heart nor means for nocturnal wanderings.

There was no doubt that a good motive inspired the orders for the nightly evacuation of the town by officers and soldiers except those actually on duty. It was thought that the Germans had discovered G.H.Q. and had resolved one night to "wipe it out." A really determined raid concentrated on a small walled town might have effected that. But the nightly march out of the troops did not impress favourably the inhabitants, who mostly had to stay. Some of them openly jeered; others made less parade of their feelings, but had them all the same.

"Where are the English?"
"The English are in the woods of Wailly."
That was a favourite street-corner gibe.

Most officers who did not get direct orders to leave the town of nights kept to their billets, but all the rank and file were marched out, or rather driven out by motor lorries. The Officers' Club closed early of evenings so that the Q.M.A.A.C.s might be evacuated to a camp outside the town. At this camp they evidently did not have the same conveniences as in the town for dressing their hair and so on; and they had to start off very early in the morning to be in time to wait at breakfast. Tempers as well as coiffures were a little ragged in consequence.

One advantage that we won from the bomb 'scare' (if that word

G. H. Q. (MONTREUIL-SUR-MER)

THE MARKET

is justified) was that it gave a stimulus to archæological research in the town. There was at G.H.Q. at the time, as a Major, R.E., that fine "sport" Professor David of Sydney University. Professor David has a great celebrity as a geologist. His birth year was 1858, so he is not exactly a youngster except in heart. But the spirit of adventure and patriotism which sent him out to the South Pole with the Shackleton Expedition in 1907-1909 sent him from Australia to this war.

He did useful work with an Australian Tunnelling Company in connection with the famous Messines mine, and his knowledge as a geologist was afterwards of great use to G.H.Q. in matters of mines, of water supply, and the like. Now he was asked to take in hand the task of providing good under-ground dug-outs for the Montreuil garrison. His researches disclosed some very interesting old galleries or quarries under the citadel.

Passages were cut through to these from points in the Ramparts, and I believe that even the good citizens of Montreuil did not disdain to take advantage of the English "dug-outs" when the German bombs began to fall.

All the same, when that nightly march out of the town was dropped we were all very glad; and our relations with the townspeople were restored to their old serenity.

At the worst the hostile section was not a very large one. Many officers who were at G.H.Q. have memories of warm personal friendships with some of the French residents, who did all that was in their power to make them feel that France was a second home. At one residence (where I was billetted for a time, that of M. Laurent and his wife) the lady had established a homely little *salon*, which was quite a student's centre not only for officers but for other ranks. Mme. Laurent spoke English well, and it was her hobby to teach French to any willing pupil of the British Army and to interest soldiers in the history of the old town. There were many others who took the same kindly interest in our mental welfare.

The good Montreuillois of 1919 certainly did not hate the English as their ancestors had done. They considered that the five years since 1914 had washed out all old injuries.

CHAPTER III.

G.H.Q. AT WORK.

The Functions of G.H.Q.—The varying conditions to be met—The working hours—The organisation of a branch—The Chief's system.

To the very end of the war, no doubt, an occasional young regimental officer could be found who knew exactly what G.H.Q. did: "They swanked about in Red Tabs and cars: had a gorgeous 'mike,' and, to keep up a show of work, issued all kinds of fool orders which nobody in the trenches had any time to read."

This theory of the functions of G.H.Q. had quite a vogue in "regimental circles" at one time. It was not, of course, founded on any mental process or it would be deeply interesting to investigate how these gentlemen came to think that ammunition and supplies could arrive fortuitously, that a concentration of troops or of Tanks could "just happen."

HAIG

LIEUT-GENERAL THE HON. SIR H. A. LAWRENCE
(Chief of the General Staff)

G. H. Q. (MONTREUIL-SUR-MER)

But, apart from that sort of thoughtless talk, there was, even among senior officers, some lack of knowledge as to what exactly the hermits of Montreuil did. They knew of them as issuing General Routine Orders in the name of the Commander-in-Chief (some 5,000 of these G.R.O.s were issued in the course of the war); as circulating, more privately, secret orders and instructions, and perhaps of making occasional appearances on the battle-field, though probably the majority of regimental officers never saw a G.H.Q. officer. In brief summary, the more important functions of G.H.Q. were:

1. G.H.Q. was the link between the B.E.F. and the British Government. The War Cabinet sitting in London was the supreme authority. The Secretary of State for War was its spokesman and, with the War Office Staff, its adviser. The Commander-in-Chief was the Army's spokesman and, with his G.H.Q., the negotiator with the Secretary of State for War. In the final result the B.E.F. had to do what it was ordered to do by the Secretary of State, but the Commander-in-Chief was usually consulted beforehand, and had always the right of discussion and of remonstrance. The relations between the Home Government and the Army were recognised as the most important matter dealt with by G.H.Q., and War Office letters had a special priority. No one except the Commander-in-Chief communicated directly with the War Office.

2. G.H.Q. was the link between the British Army in the Field and the Allied armies—the French, American, Belgian and Portuguese. Relations between these were maintained through Military Missions, we keeping a Mission with the G.H.Q. of the Allied Army, they keeping Missions with our G.H.Q. There was, quite apart from big questions of operations, discussion of which was confined to the Chief of the General Staff and the heads of the foreign Missions, an immense amount of technical transport, supply and finance work between the Allies. There was hardly an officer of G.H.Q. who did not in some detail come into relations with the foreign Missions.

3. G.H.Q. had to decide the strategy of the campaign in its relation to the British sector. After the unity of Command there was a somewhat lessened responsibility in this matter, but the work was practically the same. The Commander-in-Chief, in consultation with his Chief of Staff, his Quartermaster-General and his Adjutant-General, decided when and with what forces we should attack, when adopt a defensive policy. To come to those decisions a close and constant

study was necessary by the various branches of G.H.Q. of the state of the enemy's forces, our own numbers and *morale*, our possibilities of transport and supply.

4. G.H.Q. had to arrange the supply, from Home and from its own workshops and local civilian workshops, of all the wonderful equipment of the forces, from a Tank and a 15-inch howitzer to a tin of dubbin; all the ammunition and all the food supplies to man and beast. There came to the ports of France every month for the B.E.F. about 800,000 tons of stuff. The men to be fed totalled over 2,000,000 and the animals to be fed about 500,000. A month's supply of ammunition weighed about 260,000 tons.

5. G.H.Q. managed a transport system which used constantly about half a million horses and mules and about 20,000 motor lorries, running over 9,000,000 motor miles per month; which carried on its light railways about 544,000 tons a month and ran every day 250 trains on broad gauge lines.

6. G.H.Q. was constantly building new railways and new roads, and developing new harbour facilities. It ran big canal and sea services, forestry and agricultural services, repair shops, laundries, etc., on a gigantic scale.

7. G.H.Q managed the vast medical services for wounded and sick, the veterinary services, the laboratories for the defence of our men and animals against poison gas and for the gas counter-offensive. It was responsible for the organisation of the Chaplains' services, for educational work and the amusement of the men.

Such was the work of G.H.Q. It was carried on under these varying conditions:

1. Maintaining a stabilised position. This was comparatively easy. Wastage of men, horses and material could be calculated with some certainty and replaced by a routine process.

2. Preparing for a big attack. This made the greatest strain on Transport and Supply, and the necessary conditions of secrecy added complications and difficulties. In preparing an offensive the Traffic more than doubled per Division. The necessary making of new railways and new roads and the accumulation of defence material to fortify a new line were responsible for most of this. But the accumulation of a big head of ammunition was also a factor. On a quiet sector two Divisions could get along with about three

trains daily. For the purposes of a big attack ten Divisions might be concentrated on that sector and those ten Divisions in the preparatory stage of the attack would need about 33 supply trains a day, and during the offensive about 27 trains a day. Put the problem into terms of civil railway administration. Tell the manager of the London to Brighton line that next week he must carry 15 times the normal traffic for a number of days and that it is extremely important that people observing his termini and his lines should not notice anything unusual.

3. Resisting a big attack. The most difficult element of this was its unexpectedness. The total provision needed for it was less than for an offensive. The amount of supplies necessary to go up by train per Division from Base would be 25 percent. less than in the case of the preparation of a big attack. We always carried a good reserve stock of ammunition, food, and engineering stores close behind the line, and a further reserve of ammunition already loaded on trains at appropriate railway centres. In case of emergency, ammunition could start moving up in just the time necessary to hitch a locomotive on to a standing train. Experience of the German offensive in 1918 showed that we carried near the front line too great reserves, and we lost a good deal of food, stores and ammunition in consequence. That big attack indeed disclosed several chinks in our armour. It showed that in some cases during Trench War units had allowed themselves to become immobile. (To give one example, many Casualty Clearing Stations had burdened themselves with surgical stores and equipment which should be reserved for stationary hospitals. Thus burdened, they were tempted to evacuate too soon). There were weaknesses, too, in Ammunition Columns, and the railway system was not nearly elastic enough. But we pulled through, largely because the British officer and soldier has always a bit in reserve and never thinks so quickly or acts so bravely as when in a tight corner.

4. Carrying on a general offensive. This was the supreme test of the British Staff from August, 1918, to November, 1918. It called for an effort that put in the category of easy things all that had gone before. The effort was gloriously successful. The British Army succeeded where the German Army in 1914, under far more favourable circumstances, had failed.

I have given only the most important of the functions of G.H.Q. and a very inadequate idea of the conditions under which it had to carry on its tasks, yet for all this there were only 300 officers at Montreuil and 240 officers at the outlying directorates.

It did not leave much chance for idleness! At G.H.Q., in my time, in my branch, no officer who wished to stay was later than 9 a.m. at his desk; most of the eager men were at work before then. We left at 10.30 p.m. if possible, more often later. On Saturday and Sunday exactly the same hours were kept. "An hour for exercise" in the afternoon was supposed to be reserved, in addition to meal-hours; but it was not by any means always possible. During the worst of the German offensive in the spring of 1918 Staff officers toiled from 8.30 a.m. to midnight, with half-hour intervals for meals. I have seen a Staff officer faint at table from sheer pressure of work, and dozens of men, come fresh from regimental work, wilt away under the fierce pressure of work at G.H.Q.

The extreme character of the strain at G.H.Q. used to be recognised by a special allowance of leave. A short leave every three months was, for a long time, the rule. With pressure of work, that rule fell in abeyance, and a G.H.Q. Staff Officer was lucky to get a leave within six months. In the case of the big men at the head of the departments leave was something to be talked of, dreamt of, but never realised. Compared with conditions at G.H.Q. regimental work was care-free and pleasant.

G.H.Q. was organised in this fashion. At the head was the Commander-in-Chief and his personal staff consisting of an Assistant Military Secretary, a Private Secretary, a Medical Officer, an Officer in charge of escorts and five A.D.C.s. Attached to this personal staff were an American and a French Staff Officer. There was one officer of the Dominions on the Chief's personal staff, Captain Botha, a son of the late General Botha, Prime Minister of South Africa. With his personal staff the Commander-in-Chief was quartered at a château near Montreuil.

One rarely saw "the Chief." He seldom had occasion to come to the offices in the Ecole Militaire, and it was only the highest officers who had to go to confer with him. But his presence was always felt. There was no more loyal band of brothers than the Grand Staff of the British Army in 1918, and the humblest member at G.H.Q. expressed the spirit of the Commander-in-Chief, and, within his sphere, was trying to do exactly as the Commander-in-Chief would do. When "the Chief" did appear at Montreuil all felt they had the right to desert work for five minutes to go to a window to catch a glimpse of him as he passed from one side of the Ecole Militaire to the other, or stopped in the great courtyard to chat for a moment with one of his officers.

Under the Chief the staff was divided into branches. There was the "Military Secretary's Branch," a small branch under Major-General H. G. Ruggles-Brise, whose duties were to look after honours, promotions, etc. There was the General Staff Branch, under Lieut.-General the Hon. Sir H. A. Lawrence, divided into the Operations Section, under Major-General J. H. Davidson (having charge of the actual strategy and tactics in the campaign); the Staff Duties Section, under Major-General G. P. Dawnay; and the Intelligence Section, under Brigadier-General G. S. Clive (having charge of the collection of information as to the enemy's movements, dispositions, intentions, etc.). There was the Adjutant-General's Branch, under Lieutenant-General Sir G. H. Fowke (having charge of discipline). There was the Quartermaster-General's Branch, under Lieutenant-General Sir Travers Clarke (having charge of supply and transport). Finally there were certain officers with special duties attached to G.H.Q. but not directly under any of these branches, such as the Officer Commanding Royal Artillery, the Inspector of Machine Gun Units, the Engineer-in-Chief, the officers in charge of Mines and Searchlights, the Inspector of Training, the Chief Chaplains, the Provost Marshal, and the Deputy Judge Advocate-General.

LIEUT-GENERAL SIR G. H. FOWKE
(Adjutant-General, B.E.F.)

G. H. Q. (MONTREUIL-SUR-MER)

Of the branches of the Staff, the Quartermaster-General's was far the greatest, for under it came all the transport and supply services. This was the formidable list:

Director of Agricultural Production (Brig.-Gen. the Earl of Radnor).
Director of Army Postal Services (Brig.-Gen. Price).
Deputy Controller of E.F. Canteens (Col. E. Benson).
Director of Engineering Stores (Brig.-Gen. Sewell).
Director of Forestry (Brig.-Gen. Lord Lovat).
Director of Hirings and Requisitions, and President of Claims Commission (Major-Gen. Rt. Hon. L. B. Friend).
Controller of Labour (Brig.-Gen. Wace).
Director of Ordnance Services (Major-Gen. Sir C. M. Mathew).
Paymaster-in-Chief (Major-Gen. Sir C. A. Bray).
Director of Remounts (Brig.-Gen. Sir F. S. Garrett).
Controller of Salvage (Brig.-Gen. Gibb).
Director of Supplies (Major-Gen. Carter).
Director of Motor Transport (Major-Gen. Boyce).
Director-General of Transportation (Major-Gen. Crookshank).
Director of Veterinary Services (Major-Gen. Moore).
Vice-Chairman Imperial War Graves Commission (Major-Gen. Ware).
Director of Works (Major-Gen. Sir A. M. Stuart).

Nor does that finish the list, for subsidiary directorates under the Director-General of Transportation were:
Director of Construction (Brig.-Gen. Stewart).
Director of Docks (Brig.-Gen. Wedgewood).
Director of Inland Water Transport (Brig.-Gen. Luck).
Director of Light Railways (Brig.-Gen. Harrison).
Director of Railway Traffic (Brig.-Gen. Murray).
Director of Roads (Brig.-Gen. Maybury).

The Transportation Directorate was, so to speak, a sub-branch of the Staff. It had a great standard-gauge railway system which kept 900 locomotives running, which in one day could send 196 trains from the Bases to railheads (this irrespective of trains on lateral lines) and in one week once moved 439,801 troops and in one month 1,539,410 troops. Its railway system was constantly being pushed forward, being duplicated, and being furnished with "avoiding lines." Further, Transportation had a light railway system which carried 174,923 tons a week. Those were only two of its activities. On inland waterways, Transportation carried 293,593 tons a month, and it worked, in addition, a coastal barge traffic, a cross-Channel barge service, and a cross-Channel Ferry. Of roads, it maintained about 4,106 miles and was always making new ones; and it took 4,400 tons of material—much of it imported by sea—to make a mile of new road.

These figures are impressive enough in themselves and yet give little real sense of the full task of the Transportation Services. That can only be realised when it is kept in mind that practically all the work had to be carried out under conditions of shock and violent movement. It was not a matter of peacefully carrying on a routine business. At every point there was a constant liability to interruption and destruction by enemy action. At every hour there was some new development requiring some change of method, of destination. The vast machine had to be as elastic as it was powerful.

Yet that was only one sub-branch of the Staff.

It will be of interest to note how all the directorates of the Q Branch of the Staff were co-ordinated so that the man at the top could keep control and yet not be smothered under a mass of detail. Under the head (Lieutenant-General Sir Travers Clarke) of this Branch of the Staff were two deputies (Major-General Ford and Major-General May). Under these deputies were five Brigadier-Generals, and under them nine Lieutenant-Colonels, and these Lieutenant-Colonels divided between them 82 subjects. A table showing the distribution of these subjects was circulated throughout the Staff, and most matters got to the right officer from the beginning, and if they were of a routine nature were dealt with at once without further reference. Very important matters, or new questions arising, went up to one of the Deputies and were referred, or not, to the Q.M.G. as the circumstances dictated. Attached to the Branch and directly under its head was an officer who had charge of all orders and all publications. Nothing could be sent out as an order from the Q.M.G. Branch, or nothing printed as an instruction from the Branch, until it had gone through his hands; and it was his duty to see that one section of the Branch did not tread on the toes of another, that orders and publications did not overlap, and that an order in which several directorates were interested was drafted in accordance with the views of all of them.

Other Branches of the Staff did not call for such elaborate organisation, for their duties were not so various. But all worked on very much the same plan—of delegating authority so that once a line of action on any particular point was decided upon, a comparatively junior staff officer could "carry on" without worrying his superiors by frequent references.

A G.H.Q. officer was distinguished not only by his red staff badges but by a red and blue arm-band. An "attached officer," *i.e.,* an officer who was working with the staff as a learner or a helper and was perhaps graded for pay, etc., as a staff officer, did not wear these distinctions until he was actually appointed to the Staff.

G.H.Q. AT WORK.

THE GRANDE PLACE

G. H. Q. (MONTREUIL-SUR-MER)

The red and blue arm-band was a chromatic outrage—its glaring colours of course had a purpose—and quite spoiled the appearance of a tunic. But it was dearly prized and as a rule. was worn on leave, though it had then no usefulness. In the field the distinguishing arm-band was of great use, to indicate to officers and men the officials to whom they could appeal in case of need. There were all sorts of arm-bands with various colour symbols and initials in addition to the G.H.Q. one. A list of them will indicate the complexity of the task of a modern army in the field. Special arm-bands of different designs were authorised to distinguish:

> General Headquarters.
> Army Headquarters.
> Army Corps Headquarters.
> Corps Machine Gun Officers.
> R.A.F. Headquarters.
> Cavalry Divisional Headquarters.
> Divisional Headquarters.
> Tank Corps Staff.
> Tank Headquarters.
> Tank Brigade.
> Cavalry Brigade.
> Infantry Brigade.
> Cavalry Divisional Artillery Headquarters.
> Divisional Artillery Headquarters.
> G.H.Q. Troops Headquarters.
> Lines of Communication.
> Provost Marshal and his assistants.
> Signal Service.
> Military Police.
> Railway Transport Officers.
> Embarkation Staff.
> Staff, Directorate of Light Railways.
> Staff, Directorate of Roads.
> Staff, Directorate of Docks.
> Staff, Directorate of Transportation.
> Staff, Directorate Inland Water Transport.
> Staff, Directorate Broad Gauge Railways.
> Light Railways District Superintendent.
> Light Railways Inspector.
> Light Railways Yardmaster.

G.H.Q. AT WORK.

Light Railways Controlman.
Light Railways Guard.
Officers, Staff Inspector War Trophies.
Servants to Military Attaches.
Stretcher bearers.
All medical personnel.
Press correspondents and servants.
Train Conducting Officers.
Checkers.
Town Majors.
Traffic Control.
Agents de Police Special.
Instructors of Machine Gun School, Lewis Gun School, and Machine Gun Corps Base Depôt.
H.Q. Corps Heavy Artillery.
Special Brigade.
Area Commandants.
Billet and Camp Wardens.
Corps Chemical Advisers.
Divisional Gas Officers.
Instructors of Divisional Gas Schools.
Camouflage Officers attached to Corps.
Salvage Corps.
Civilian Platelayers.
Intelligence Police.
Sanitary Sections.
Belgian Civ. Rly. Staff.
M.L.O. Staff at Ports.
N.C.O.s and men of Intelligence Corps.
N.C.O.s and men of Dock Directorate.
Sentries on Examining Posts.
Interpreters, Indian Labour Corps.
Interpreters, Chinese Labour Corps.

The Military Police were supposed to be able to keep all these in memory and an officer in the field had to know the chief ones; and he took care to know at least that for G.H.Q., for it represented the ultimate source of honour and blame. Nothing important could happen to him except through G.H.Q., and that ugly red and blue arm-band always demanded attention, sometimes, no doubt, mixed with a little resentment, because of the idea that G.H.Q. had nothing much to do except to bother the unhappy regimental officer.

We all tried to "live up to" our arm-bands in the crude stained-glass-window colours. The Commander-in-Chief set a high example by choosing his men carefully, giving them their particular jobs and trusting them. He was not one of those fussy souls who want to oversee every detail. The men who worked under him knew that whilst they did their work conscientiously and carefully he would back them against any niggling criticism and against any back-biting. It was a good policy judged by its results. G.H.Q., B.E.F., France, in the summer of 1918 had probably reached as high a summit of soldierly scientific skill as the grand Staff of any Army in the world. The business of improvisation which had been begun in 1914 was finished, actually finished. From G.H.Q. was directed day by day a fighting force which met the chief brunt of the last German attack, held it; then, while it absorbed a great flood of recruits and helped to equip and train the American Army, prepared to take the chief part in the final victorious offensive.

CHAPTER IV.

G.H.Q. AT PLAY.

The walks on the Ramparts—The "Monks" of Montreuil had little time for sport—Precautions against "joy-riding"—The jolly Officers' Club—Watching the Map—Ladies at G.H.Q.?

THERE was precious little play-time at G.H.Q. But there was some. It was spent very innocently; not to say stodgily. A walk on the Ramparts was the chief recreation of the great majority of the officers.

What a boon those Ramparts were! Within a minute from the Ecole Militaire one could get on the broad walk which crowned the old walls and could follow it round the whole circuit of the town for a mile or more. From every point there was a rich and ample prospect; southward over the swelling downs and little copses towards the forest of Crécy; westward over a richer and more luxuriant plain towards the sea; northward across the woods and marshes of the Canche; eastward along the valley of the river and its bordering hills. On a fine day at the coming up and the going down of the sun, and every hour between, there was a constant festival of light and colour. Stormy and rainy skies gave another beauty to the wide prospect. To see a storm march up in grand procession and pass with its sombre pomp was a fearful joy; and there was a wild beauty, too, in looking out from the walls on the beating of the obstinate rains against hill and plain. Painters from all over the world used to come to Montreuil to attempt to put on canvas the glow of its summer scenes, the wild grandeur of its winters. No day was without its special beauty, and the beauty was ever renewed afresh.

In the early spring the chinks and crannies of the old walls burst into bloom of gillyflowers which hung them with tapestries of gold and red and brown, contrasting gaily with the bright green foliage of the trees growing at the base of the Ramparts and throwing their branches up to their very top. As the season advanced the birds came to build in the trees, and you might peep down into their nests and hear their indignant chirrups at being so closely overlooked. With summer and autumn came new colours, but always splendour and glow and movement. The country around carried that wide variety of crops in which the French peasant's thrifty and careful culture delights. There were beans and oats and wheat and corn and flax and mustard and bits of pasturage, and of fodder crops, weaving their many colours into a delightful carpet pattern which changed with every day of the year and almost with every hour of the day.

THE RAMPARTS

G. H. Q. (MONTREUIL-SUR-MER)

Had it not been for those Rampart walks the toilsome life of G.H.Q. at Montreuil would have been hardly possible. The road from anywhere to anywhere, if time allowed, was by the Ramparts. Going from the Ecole Militaire to the Officers' Club was three minutes by the street, seven minutes by the Ramparts, and most went by the Ramparts unless work was hideously pressing. For those with a little more time to spare there were enchanting rambles around the base of the Ramparts along the Canche valley or in the old fosses of the fortifications.

Riding was not a common exercise. Horses were scarce. Very few officers had their own chargers; and those who had could not find time to exercise them properly. So most of the horses at G.H.Q. were pooled, and an officer having time and inclination took what horse was available. There were many pleasant rides, the favourite one being a shady stretch along the bank of the river.

At one point of the fortifications an old fosse had been converted into hard tennis courts, and these were used a little, but not much. It seems tiresome to be always repeating the same fact but really there was not time to follow tennis or any other sport. At the Officers' Club there was not such a thing as a billiard table; and I never saw a game of cards played there. In some of the private messes there was a feeble attempt to keep up a Bridge or a Poker circle. But to begin to play at cards at 11 p.m. with the knowledge that the office is calling for a clear rested brain by nine the next morning, needs far more than ordinary enthusiasm. I can remember playing cards only three nights during all my time at Montreuil.

There was a theatre at Montreuil, usually given up to cinema shows but occasionally visited by the variety companies which were organised for the amusement of the troops and occasionally also converted into a lecture hall. It was well patronised on special occasions, but in the course of a year made little total demand on officers' time. When, as was usually the case, the theatre was given up to "the pictures" it was filled by "other ranks." The non-commissioned officers and privates who were clerks in the various departments had generally just as little leisure as their officers, but some of the military population had more time to spare; what section I do not know, for even the grooms and the batmen had not easy places. Officers junior to the rank of lieutenant-colonel were not allowed a batman to themselves, but one soldier acted for two or three officers and had various fatigue duties.

THE THEATRE

G. H. Q. (MONTREUIL-SUR-MER)

Just outside the town, G.H.Q. Recreation Ground provided a lumpy football ground and a still more lumpy cricket ground. Both our national games languished, however, for the stock reason—want of time. There were teams, and occasional matches, and sometimes an enthusiastic sportsman would send an urgent whip round to call attention to our deplorable neglect of the games that made England great. He would get a few half-hearted promises of reform, but there was no hope in fighting against the great obstacle. It was like a college in which every one was a "swotter."

So the 300 or so Monks of Montreuil lived their laborious lives. The balance of G.H.Q. staff, some 250, scattered about the environs of Montreuil with their offices at Paris Plage or Le Touquet or the Forest of Crécy, could follow a somewhat milder discipline. They were "Second Echelon" mostly. Current operations had not much concern for them and it was possible to take horse-back exercise, to keep up football and cricket and even tennis and golf. At Le Touquet, which was a well-known pleasure centre before the war, there were good golf links and some excellent tennis courts. On occasions the Commander-in-Chief decided to think out his problems over a round of golf, and a little bungalow was maintained at Le Touquet for his convenience.

Paris Plage was a splendid beach, but so far as G.H.Q. officers were concerned its attractions were wasted. Occasionally an officer having business at one of the Directorates near by would spare an hour for a swim, but it was not possible on a hot Saturday or Sunday to suspend the battle, or the preparation for the battle, in progress and adjourn as a body to the seaside. Not only time but transport was lacking. The only means of getting down to the beach—a distance of about twelve miles—was by motor-car, and regulations against "joy-riding" were strict. Not only were there regulations; there were also precautions to see that the regulations were kept. A car could go out from G.H.Q. garage only on an order from the officer in charge of cars, and it was his business to get a chit as to what was the reason for the journey. Occasionally police patrols would be stationed on the roads with instructions to stop every car and examine its papers. This was excused as a precaution against espionage. It was designed more to be a precaution against waste of petrol or "joy-riding," as a few officers found to their cost.

So the life of the Montreuil officer resolved itself ordinarily into this simple routine: he worked and he walked on the Ramparts. But there was one fine relief to tedium for the majority—a dinner-party every night. The big generals, because they had to, and a few unwise souls, because they chose to, favoured private messes and confronted at dinner at night the same men as they met in the office all day; and, without a doubt, found it rather monotonous. The majority of the officers messed at the Officers' Club, which had a couple of hundred members and could rival the old reputation of the House of Commons as "the finest Club in Europe."

The qualification for joining the Officers' Club was to be an officer of the British Army or of an Allied Army stationed at Montreuil. The subscription was five francs per month, and for that and a ridiculously small sum per day the Club gave members three square meals a day and afternoon tea. The Club kept up a good cellar, and to the very last, when good wine was almost unprocurable in London or Paris except at exorbitant prices, the Officers' Club, Montreuil, could sell a vintage claret or burgundy at nine francs a bottle, a decent wine at five francs a bottle, and champagne at fifteen francs a bottle. The Expeditionary Force Canteens were the caterers, and aimed at only a nominal profit. Once a week there was a fixed guest night and a band, but members could bring guests at any time. Waiting was done by Q.M.A.A.C.s, neat deft little ladies who brought a hint of home to the exiles.

Custom was against forming coteries. So there were constantly differing dinner-parties, and the conversation was rich in variety and interest. The backbone of the Mess were the Regular Army officers, the majority of them colonels, with a sprinkling of brigadiers, a few majors and a few captains. The majority in the Mess, however, were temporary officers, a few of senior rank, mostly staff captains or attached officers. There were always some visitors, a politician or some other personage from home, staff officers from the War Office or from the various Armies, regimental officers having business at G.H.Q., guests from the various private messes at Montreuil.

Talk ranged from the most serious shop to the most airy nothings. There were experts there in almost every department of human knowledge, men who had seen many cities and known the minds of many men. The representatives of the Allied nations gave an extra note of variety. You might sit at the same table with an American one night, an Italian another, or a Frenchman or Belgian or Portuguese. The majority of men present were distinguished men either in the Service or in some civil profession or business. Travel, science, art and literature, were all well represented.

IN THE OFFICERS' CLUB

G.H.Q. AT PLAY.

Smoking was prohibited in the Officers' Club until a certain hour, and the Q.M.A.A.C. waitresses had no difficulty in seeing that the rule was kept by all ranks. At an earlier date, when a sergeant-major with men orderlies had charge of the waiting, discipline on this point was not so easily maintained. Any junior officer lighting up before the hour was promptly checked. But a sergeant-major found it difficult to take "disciplinary action" against an officer of General rank. One evening a very lofty general indeed, a visitor to the Mess, started a huge cigar at 8 o'clock. Smoking was not allowed until 8.20. The sergeant-major was a man of resource. Bringing in a ladder, he mounted to the Mess clock and solemnly set it on to 8.20. A General was smoking, therefore it must be 8.20.

As I have said, they fed us very well at the Mess. But of course we grumbled at the food and found one point of criticism in the fish. Montreuil being practically a seaside town, the fish was naturally not good, authority having transferred to this English colony in France the invariable tradition of British seaside resorts to send all the fresh fish away and consume the refuse. Our fish was always plaice, and it was often plaice that had known better days. One wag spoke of it as the "vintage plaice," professed to know that it had been "laid down" the year the war started, and that the "bins" would not be exhausted until the war ended.

But the plaice was never a really serious grievance. It gave opportunity, but not valid cause, to grumble, and discussion of it died away after an officer one night quoted mock heroically:

> Ah, friend—had this indubitable fact
> Haply occurred to poor Leonidas
> How had he turned tail on Thermopulai!
> It cannot be that even his few wits
> Were addled to the point that, so advised,
> Preposterous he had answered—"Cakes are prime,
> Hearth-sides are snug, sleek dancing-girls have worth,
> And yet for country's sake, to save our gods
> Their temples, save our ancestors their tombs,
> Save wife and child and home and liberty,—I
> would chew sliced-salt-fish, bear snow—nay, starve
> If need were—and by much prefer the choice!"

After dinner the routine was to go and look at the map before settling down again to work. Military Intelligence, in one of its rooms, kept up-to-date hour-by-hour a map of the fighting front, and after dinner we would crowd to this room to see the latest official news put up on the map and to hear the latest unofficial stories which embroidered the news. One evening, as a great advance on our part was marked up on the map, the clerk, moving the flag-pins, announced:

"They say the enemy cleared out so quickly that they left the hospitals behind, and the Australian corps has captured 50 German nurses. They report that they are looking well after them."

A titter went round the group of officers. It happened to be the night after the story had circulated—a story which President Wilson has since adopted among his family of anecdotes—that the Australians, having the Americans to co-operate with, had had to remonstrate with them for their undue rudeness to the Germans. The Australians had a reputation for being quite direct enough in their method of teaching the Boche not to be a Boche.

The titter, perhaps, had an injurious inference to some ears, for a General officer remarked, a little sternly:

"Gentlemen, the Australians are a gallant race. The German—er—ladies will be quite safe with them."

So, of course, it proved. It was fiction that any Colonial troops showed an undue sternness to prisoners. The average German knew that he was quite safe in the hands of any British unit—whether it was from Australia, Canada, or the Motherland.

The after-dinner peep at the map was a great finish to dinner. When the Armistice was signed officers were disconsolate for the loss of their ten minutes in the M.I. room. "I miss," said one, "our pleasant daily habit of advancing ten kilomètres on a front of fifty kilomètres." No, life at G.H.Q. was sober and strenuous, but it was not dull or tedious. If a man has good work to do, lovely aspects of Nature to look upon, interesting company at his meals, he has all the real essentials of contentment; well, most of them.

Ladies at G.H.Q.? An almost accurate chapter might be written on this point on the lines adopted in that exhaustive and conscientious book on Iceland, which had a brief chapter:

The Snakes of Iceland.
There are no snakes in Iceland.

There were no ladies at G.H.Q., not at any rate in the sense that would be in the mind of the average inquirer. On the too rare occasions when I was able to get a leave from G.H.Q., or was sent over to London on a task, the civilians I encountered in London exhibited a considerable interest in the ladies that were thought to haunt G.H.Q.

This was by no manner of means an entirely or indeed a mainly feminine curiosity. Many people have an ineradicable idea that an Army on a campaign ravages the hearts of all the female population of the occupied territory, as well as drawing on the beauty of its own land to recruit charming camp followers. I can recall, on returning from a small war some time before 1914, attending a dinner-party in London and being tremendously flattered at the fact that as soon as the ladies went upstairs all the men (some of them very distinguished men) crowded round me in a spirit of inquiry. With all the resources at my disposal I framed in my mind a brief and vivid appreciation of the campaign. But—they did not want to know why the Turkish Army failed or the Serbian Army succeeded. Someone rather well known in London had got into a scrape in the course of the campaign, and there were some very scandalous details alleged. My eager inquirers wanted to know all those scandalous details, and were obviously disappointed to learn that there was no reasonable foundation for them, and at once lost all interest in the campaign. My "appreciation" had not the chance to be uttered.

Probably they concluded I was rather an unintelligent person not to have discovered all the horrid details. Certainly those to whom I told the truth about the ladies and G.H.Q. thought I was either very sly or very unobservant. Indeed one very hearty old gentleman, with a great passion for horrid details, patted me on the back publicly. "That's right, that's right. I admire you for sticking to your friends. But of course we do not believe you."

Categorically, it is *not* a fact that "beautiful leaders of British society" constantly graced G.H.Q. with their presence. In the very early stages of the war some of the "Smart Set" considered it rather the thing to get over to the battlefields and make a week-end sensation of a glimpse at the Calvary of Civilisation. They usually got over through the influence of political friends, and most often by way of the Belgian section of the Front, which was not so sternly guarded as the British or French sections. Military authority discountenanced these visits—however "fashionable" and beautiful the visitors—and soon put a stop to them. After 1914, except nurses and Q.M.A.A.C.s it was very rare for a woman to enter British Army areas. Those few who did come had very definite business and were expected to attend very strictly to that business and then to move off.

There was a suspicion that some few, a very few, "workers" were in France not so much for work as because they found it amusing. These got no further than the Base ports as a rule, and were not officially encouraged. The vast majority of the women workers in France were there for patriotism's sake, attended strictly to their business, and had no time (or inclination, presumably) for frivolity.

All this is very disappointing, I am aware. But it is true. The life we lived at G.H.Q. was truly monastic. We never saw an English woman unless she were a nurse or Q.M.A.A.C. or some other uniformed fellow-officer or fellow-soldier.

G.H.Q. AT PLAY.

THE PLACE GAMBETTA

G. H. Q. (MONTREUIL-SUR-MER)

Nor was there any idle local feminine society to take the thoughts of officers from the stern tasks of war. Montreuil was very, very prim and dull even for a small French provincial town. There may still be some people whose ideas of French social life are based on those quarters of Paris whose theatres, books, newspapers, restaurants, manners are shaped by the wishes (or fancied wishes) of the floating population of visitors and of a small section of idle and worthless French. But I fancy that in these days such people are few; and most people know that the average of French life is not at all like Montmartre or the Latin Quarter, which are less typical of France than, say, Piccadilly Circus is of England. For thorough straight-laced respectability there is nothing to beat a small French provincial town. Montreuil was the most respectable place one could imagine before the war. It sheltered a small colony of artists in the summer, attracted by the wonderful panoramas from the ramparts; but they came to work, and did not bring with them what is supposed to be the atmosphere of the Latin Quarter. The local population was exceedingly decorous and rather inclined to be clerical in sympathy, for Montreuil was a great centre for schools.

During our occupation of the town as the home of G.H.Q. there might be noted occasionally the arrival from Paris, or elsewhere, of some gay young lady or couple of ladies who, having heard that the British Army had its headquarters there, had decided, from motives of patriotism, of *camaraderie*, or from less admirable motives, to come and enliven the dullness of the place. Departure would follow with ungallant promptitude. The same day, or the next, the lady would move away, with a gendarme to see that she did not miss her train.

The monastic severity of life at G.H.Q. relaxed a little, I think, when the immediate environs of Montreuil were passed. Then you had got out of the area of First Echelon G.H.Q. and were in that of the Second Echelon, which was largely made of subsidiary services not so directly concerned with the administration of the fighting Army. Life was a little less strenuous, and perhaps Aphrodite was not altogether neglected for Ares. Here conditions reflected the average attitude of the British Army administration in the matter of morals, which was practically that of British civilian life, with somewhat more precaution and guardianship but no grandmotherly supervision. The female personnel of the Army was very carefully safeguarded. The male personnel, if it were absolutely bent on it, could find opportunities for mischief in some of the Base towns. G.H.Q. itself—partly perhaps because of the necessity of extreme safeguards against espionage— was expected to lead a strictly single life; to conform to the perfect standard that was supposed to rule in the Provost Marshal's branch. That rigour, of course, was dictated not by an exceptional prudery in the P.M. authorities but by military convenience. Ordinarily, outside of G.H.Q. and the Provost Marshal's branch, there was a margin allowed for human error.

Paris Plage, the jolly beach at the mouth of the Canche near Montreuil, was for a long time "out-of-bounds" to all British troops. Paris Plage had, in pre-war days, rather a "Montmartre" reputation in Paris. It was the beach for the cheap tripper. It was the beach to which the hardworking *bourgeois* of the city who had to stick to his bureau during the summer sent his wife, and came down to see her on Sundays. It was also the beach for the Don Juan of modest means to visit with his temporary Juanita. Not this Paris reputation reacting on the traditional British hypocrisy caused the long-standing ban on Paris Plage, but practical sanitary reasons. It had not then a good reputation from the point of view of health. But as the size and the activities of G.H.Q. increased and it was necessary to find places for new departments near Montreuil, Paris Plage had to be utilised. After being subjected to a drastic sanitary inquisition it was thrown open to the troops and became the headquarters of several minor departments.

But of course the old gay life did not return. It was no longer a suburb of Montmartre. Still it preserved a certain air of rakishness. Going through there in a car one day with another staff officer we noticed a little shop in the windows of which were displayed very coquettishly two or three filmy articles of feminine *dessous*. A lightning glance through the door showed that there was quite a bevy of fair shop assistants—about three assistants to each item of merchandise. In the window there was this simple device, in English:

CHEQUES CASHED.

We dared not investigate further. A G.H.Q. car is so clearly recognisable as such that it could not stop outside, and the subterfuge of drawing up at the Directorate of Inkstands and making a reconnaissance on foot we felt to be *infra dig*. It was only possible to pass the shop slowly on the return journey, and to look out for it the next month when going that way again. It was still open, still bore its artless device. It was a little bit of the old life of Paris Plage that had escaped the shocks of war.

In very truth we were a dull lot from one point of view. Even the conversation at meals was ordinarily wanting in that type of anecdote which—as Walpole said when he was asked why it was rife at his table, where sat the greatest men of Europe, who should have had something better to talk about—is popular "because every man understands it." Perhaps the propriety of our conversation was partly due to the fact that there was nearly always a padre within earshot. Perhaps I may dare the explanation of the general absence of "sex interest" in our lives, that here were gathered together a band of men with very exacting and very important work to do, and that they simply had not time nor inclination to bother about what is usually an amusement of idle lives.

CHAPTER V.

THE MUNITIONS OF THE WAR.

The Shell shortage—When relief came—The dramatic Tanks—Bombs—Some ammunition figures—The ingenious inventor.

A S soon as any subject is involved in political discussion the facts about it are apt to be distorted in the interests of some particular view. The "Shell shortage" in the early stages of the war has become in a sense a political issue; and that I do not intend to discuss. But some facts about munitions supply must be given—for that was the very pivot of the war—irrespective of what political case they help or harm.

The British Force at the outset of the war suffered from a shell and gun shortage as compared with its enemy, because it had been trained and equipped for a different type of warfare from that which actually came. It had very little high explosive shell, and what it had was rarely "high explosive" in the real sense of the term. The patient search for a foolproof fuse had been so successful that our H.E. shell was comparatively inoffensive when it reached the enemy's lines. It spluttered off rather than shattered off. All this was put right in time. But the difficulties which the Munitions Supply Department had to face at the outset were enormous. There were, considered in the lights of the needs of this war, practically no shells, no guns, and no machinery for making them. Essential material was lacking in many cases, and the only source of quick supply was Germany, which alone in the world had organised for war.

But all difficulties were overcome. How great the growth some comparative figures will show. The production of high explosive in 1914 was almost negligible. The year's supply would not keep the guns of 1918 going for a day. In 1915 we began to produce high explosive on a large scale, and in amounts which made the 1914 output seem contemptible, but still in quite inadequate quantities. In 1916 we had increased the 1915 amount sevenfold. In 1917 we had increased that 1916 amount fourfold. From March, 1915, to March, 1917, the increase was twenty-eight fold. Of machine-guns we made samples in 1914 and we began to manufacture quantities in 1915. In 1917 we made twenty times as many as in 1915. Of aeroplanes the figures mounted in steep flights. In 1916 we seemed to be producing vastly. In 1917 the rate of production for the first six months had increased fourfold as compared with the previous year, and another great acceleration was in progress.

In the end we were enormously superior to any other Army in the field in the matter of munitions. To the very day of the Armistice improvements in the quality and rate of productions were still going on in preparation for the Spring, 1919, campaign, which it was anticipated would end the war. The German threw up the sponge before then. If he had waited he would have been literally blown out of his trenches and his chief cities.

In one sense, of course, we never had enough, but if I were asked to name a date on which a serious shortage of munitions ceased I should say September 19th, 1915, on the eve of the battle of Loos. On that date, a year after Trench War began, word was passed around to the batteries of the British line in a phrase copied from the provision shops of London: "Ammunition is cheap to-day." Every gun-pit stocked up with shell. The gates of the dumps were opened and shell fairly poured out. Battery Commanders, who knew the days when one shell per gun per day was the limit allowed, saw with joy thousands of shells, and, as they began eagerly to fire them off, thousands more coming.

On the 23rd of September a regular bombardment of the whole German line facing the British line began. The artillery was undertaking the preliminary work of wire-cutting and parapet pounding. The 18-pounders with shrapnel, the howitzers with high explosive, started at dawn, and all through the day systematically smashed away at the German's defences. That went on for two more days. The fourth day we intensified our shell-fire. Along many sections of the Front the German wire was down, and the parapet of the German trench breached. The enemy increased his artillery fire, too, attacking our trenches and searching for our observing stations and batteries, but on the whole getting the worst of the artillery duel. On the morning of the 25th the final artillery duel began. It was the greatest artillery bombardment in history up to that date, though afterwards so eclipsed by the records of the Somme, the Ancre and of Messines as to be remembered as a mere splutter. But at the time it was vastly impressive.

The morning was dull but the flashes of guns were so continuous as to give a light which was almost unbroken. It flickered, but it never failed. The earth itself quivered and shook with the repeated shocks of the guns. The air became a tattered hunted thing, torn wisps of it blown hither and thither by the constant explosions.

The Battle of Loos did not give us the break-through we expected, but, in so far as my observation is worth anything, the reason was not lack of munitions. Loos showed that the task was a more complicated one than merely smashing down the front line of enemy trenches. "Trench War" was resumed, whilst the British Army prepared for the next phase opening in July, 1916, with the first Battle of the Somme. By then munitions supply had grown gigantically and in the mechanics of war we were far ahead of the Germans. This was not only in artillery but in infantry equipment and in our unique weapon the "Tank," which was the mechanical contrivance having the most decisive results on the issue of the war. These appeared in September, 1916, two years after "Trench War" had begun, and were ultimately destined to make that sort of war impossible, a task which the German poison gas had failed to accomplish.

As a race we are never consciously dramatic, or I would have imagined on that September 1916 morning that the arrival of the Tanks on the Somme front had been carefully timed and stage-managed. The morning was dull and misty. Over the seared and terrible land little wisps of fog rose and fell. All likeness to our gentle mother earth had been battered out of the fields, which were rubbish-heaps of churned-up débris of bodies, dust, weapons—hideously pock-marked by the eruption of the shells. Where had been villages were dirtier patches of desolation. Where had been woods, groups of splintered stumps. It was an abomination of desolation, like as when the earth was first formed out of the void. In the midst of this desolation out of the mist came, crawling uncouthly, the Tanks, like prehistoric saurians.

The German forces were obviously frightened by the Tanks, which climbed over their trenches, and impervious to rifle bullets, smashed up machine-gun emplacements and redoubts. But that Tank of 1916 was nothing like the perfected machine of 1918. Its rear steering wheel was a weak-spot liable to be shot away. Its pace was too slow for it to keep up with charging infantry. No real tactics had been evolved for its use.

G. H. Q. (MONTREUIL-SUR-MER)

But, such as it was, that Tank at first brought alarm to more than the enemy. In going to and from the battle front it "got the wind up" many a British dug-out. Here is an artillery officer's yarn of the first "Tank night":

"Our 'Mess' was a roofed-over shell-hole a mile or so in front of Martinpuich. The roof would keep out shrapnel bits but was no use against a direct hit from a shell. I was Orderly Dog for the night and it was my business to take action, when, outside, a strange spluttering, growling, scratching, spitting sound broke into the steady barking of the guns. It was like a thousand cats, a hundred dogs, and a sea-sick elephant or two scrambling and squabbling together in a dust-hole. I went to investigate. A Tank wandering home was within ten yards of our Mess, heading straight for it. With all the *insouciance* I could command at such a crisis I begged the Tank to stop; urged that our roof was designed to keep out splinters only and was neither shell-proof nor Tank-proof; pointed out that if it persisted in its course seven artillery officers, some of whom had wives and children, and all of whom had mothers, would be pulped. Then I became calmer and told the Tank that there was some wine in the Mess and even some whisky and soda, if the Tank would now stop and have a drink. Fortunately a Tank is a slow mover and my cooler arguments had effect by the time it had got within five yards of our roof-tree. Then it backed water and we were safe. The Tank is a noble animal, but it adds a little to the anxieties of life underground."

THE FOSSE

G. H. Q. (MONTREUIL-SUR-MER)

"The Tank" was the great mechanical find of the war, and it was an all-British find. High authority had many fine name-proposals for the useful monsters, but Tommy took the matter into his own hands and coined the word "Tank," and "Tank" it remained. Those who are interested in matters of language may note that the French do not use the word "Tank" but describe a "Tank" as a *char d'assaut*, which is accurate, but has a weak look. It is an illustration of their jealous and admirable care of their language. They will not allow foreign words to intrude if that can be avoided. We, on the other hand, are quite careless about our language. The orders of our Army in France were bespattered with French words and phrases for which there were quite good English equivalents. (*Gare régulatrice* for "distributing station" is one of the many scores of cases in point.) It is a pity that we are so careless in regard to our mother tongue. I made an effort once to persuade G.H.Q. that British Army orders and instructions should be put out in English without any foreign admixture, but met with little sympathy. The intrusion of French words was not so bad, but German words had an almost equal degree of hospitality.

———————————————

But to return to our munitions. The hand bomb was a weapon which by 1914 we had allowed to fall out of use. The British Grenadiers no longer threw grenades. But Trench War brought back the bomb as a weapon, and our bomb was soon better than the German bomb. At the first Somme battle (1916) we showed a definite superiority in bomb supply and bomb use. This development was altogether in our favour. The bomb—beastly weapon as it is, and beastly as are the wounds it inflicts—lends its favour to the quicker brain, the prompter courage, the keener leadership. The football field and the cricket green both give a good foundation for the murderous art of bombing. As soon as we had the bombs our bombing superiority grew with every day.

An instance to illustrate bombing: For the taking of the village of Contalmaison (1916) a preliminary task was the capture of Horse Shoe trench. The attack on this was prospering when it was held up at a critical point by the unmasking of a German machine gun on our right flank. To the fire of this gun we were fully exposed, and its effect was murderous. A young cricketer rose to the occasion. Single-handed he rushed the gun with a bagful of bombs, got to his distance and destroyed it with a couple of 'hot returns from the outfield'. In

THE MUNITIONS OF THE WAR.

using ammunition the B.E.F. put up some startling records. On August 8th, 1918, when our big final thrust began there were used 15,598 tons in a single day. On September 29th, 1918, there were used 23,706 tons. Here are some other big figures:

Date.	Battle	Amount	
1/7/16	Somme	12,776	tons
9/4/17	Vimy	24,706	″
3/6/17	Arras	17,162	″
7/6/17	Messines	20,638	″
31/7/17	Ypres	22,193	″
20/9/17 } 21/9/17 }	Polygon Wood	42,156	″

In the depôts in France we kept a reserve of 258,000 tons of ammunition, and the issues in a normal month ran to about that figure though it varied a good deal month by month. Thus the average expenditure during the last months of 1918 was: May, 5,478 tons daily; June, 4,748 tons daily; July, 5,683 tons daily; August, 9,046 tons daily; September, 8,576 tons daily; October, 4,748 tons daily; November, 3,158 tons daily. On November 11th, the last day of the war, we used 233 tons of ammunition.

Different varieties of ammunition had widely different rates of use. The gigantic 15-inch howitzer on some days did not fire a single round. It was a "big day" when it fired fifty rounds. It was just as well that it was not a gun which indulged in thousands of rounds, for a ten-ton broad-gauge railway truck would only take twelve rounds for it. The 18-pounder field guns would shoot 100,000 rounds on a normal day, and on a heavy day would use 200,000 rounds. The cost of ammunition was, in a time of heavy fighting, up to £3,000,000 *per day.*

A heavy item in munitions was for defence against poison gas and for our own poison gas service. We entered with extreme reluctance into the ghastly business, but once we started we soon made the German sorry that he had brought that element into the war. Our gases were more potent and more plentiful than his. For lack of material he could not give his men perfect gas protectors, while to our men we could and did.

The last loathsome trick of the enemy in this direction was the introduction of mustard gas, a powerful corrosive which was discharged from shells. The use of mustard gas by the enemy raised a number of problems for Supplies as apart from the Medical Staffs. The disinfection with chloride of lime of ground contaminated with the gas, a prompt change of clothing and bath treatment for men affected, proved efficacious in dealing with mustard gas. There was, too, safety in protective overalls of oilskin. Mustard gas affected the Veterinary Service heavily, there being many casualties to horses and mules through passing over ground infected with the gas.

The inventive spirit was naturally strong in the Army, and some of the most useful of the new ideas in the way of munitions or equipment came from men in the Field. These ideas were tested in the Army workshops, and occasionally there was a certain amount of waste owing to the same idea, or nearly the same idea, being experimented with simultaneously in more than one Army. So an Army Order from Home recalled the King's Regulation that War Office approval must be obtained before experimental work was done in regard to any invention. But this, it was urged from G.H.Q., would act prejudicially to the interests of the Force in France, since many very useful inventions regarding stores and material had come from officers and men of the Force and it was not in the best interests of the public to put any obstacles in the way of future inventions. This was recognised, and a subsequent Army Order gave authority to the Commander-in-Chief of any Expeditionary Force to authorise trials of inventions; but precautions were taken in regard to duplication and overlapping.

There were not in the Field so many foolish inventors as at Home. No such merry idea came to G.H.Q. as that anti-submarine device with which the Admiralty was plagued—a liquid air shell which on being exploded anywhere in the vicinity of a submarine formed an extensive iceberg (through the lowering of the surrounding temperature by a release of the liquid air from pressure). On this iceberg the submarine would be brought to the surface. The next step would be easy: open with an oyster knife, sprinkle with pepper and salt and a dash of lemon juice, and serve.

The B.E.F. had never anything quite so naive as that. Its limit was the inventor who claimed to be able to project an X-ray from an electric battery so that it would kill anything within 1,000 yards. This invention would have been a great war-stopper. It would have been only necessary to set up a sufficient number of the projectors along our Front, switch on the current and march on to Berlin. It was offered at a time when inventions were rather the fashion, and it needed courage to scoff at even the most curious notion. So it actually got to the stage of a trial with a High Authority present. The inventor set up his projector; an animal was let loose within its deadly range and, surely enough, dropped dead. Unfortunately for the inventor a medical scoffer subjected the animal to a *post mortem* examination and found that it had evidently resolved on suicide, for it had taken a large dose of strychnine. This discouraged further trials of the X-ray device.

The inventor with a "wireless" device for exploding enemy magazines also cropped up. You projected a wireless ray and it blew up a dump. This invention could be very convincingly demonstrated within your own lines. All that was necessary was to provide in the dump a certain amount of loose explosive, a fulminate, and a receiver tuned to receive your wireless message. We were not on sufficiently good terms with the Germans to persuade them to arrange their ammunition depôts in this way for our convenience.

There was a close *liaison* kept up between the B.E.F. and the Ministry of Munitions. When Mr. Winston Churchill was Minister of Munitions he was over in France so frequently that a small château was kept up for him at G.H.Q. He was wont to come into the Officers' Club for his meals. There was always an air about him that he would have liked to be in the jack-boots of his famous ancestor and give the world a spectacle of another Marlborough winning victories in Flanders.

CHAPTER VI.

THE MEDICAL SERVICES.

The magic-workers of the war—Fighting the Germans—
Concerning the Victorian primness of conversation and the
present popularity of "v.d." as a theme for small talk—The
Army and "v.d."—The etiquette of hospitals and the ways
of matrons—The war against Trench Feet—Mustard gas in
1918.

P ROBABLY more than half the men at G.H.Q. had been "crocked"
at one time or another during the campaign, from wounds or
one of those fevers of the battlefield born of mud and filth and
fatigue. Some came to work on the Staff whilst still under medical
treatment, and there was a local hospital at Montreuil which was a
boon to those out-patients needing massage for their scars or quinine
for their fevers.

Apart from the doctors of this hospital only the very big men of
the medical services appeared ever at G.H.Q. It was a pleasure not
easily won to persuade them to talk over their work. But when they
did talk, what wonders they had to tell of!

A BY-WAY

Socrates in prison, when the fetters were taken off his legs, as he rubbed them to make the blood run freely again, speculated on how pleasure always followed pain, so that the two seemed to be linked together by some unbreakable bond. One would like to hear Socrates to-day, as his limb, injured in Flanders, was rubbed back to usefulness, talking to his masseur on the good that will follow the evil of the Great War as surely as if the two had been linked together and one was the consequence of the other. Matter for a fine homily there from the stubborn old hero with the divinely clear mind!

Those optimists who thought that a new heaven and a new earth would come at the end of the war, and that even all politicians would become sincere, alert, and vigorous in the public service, were perhaps not reasonable and may be disappointed in some measure; but no one can observe closely the phenomena of the war without being sure that from its sacrifices and lessons much good will come. The dreadful fire that had to be kindled to burn out the cancer of Germanism burned out evil too in the nations that were the instruments of vengeance. Peoples who went into war iron will come out steel ultimately; for the war, as well as being preservative, will prove regenerative. There is no better proof of this than in the tale of our campaigns against the germs, those pitiless enemies who are always attacking human content and happiness. It was a wonderful part of the war, that defensive and offensive against Disease, with its trench systems which hold up foes whom we cannot destroy with our present weapons; its Intelligence Department, spying with a thousand microscopes into the designs and dispositions of the enemy; its clever diplomatic service, always raising up allies in our blood against germ invasion; its long illustrious roll of heroes who have given up life or health to hold positions against odds or to go out on forlorn hopes.

In this the benefits springing out from the Great War show splendid and palpable. In the process of beating the Germans we made such great advances in the war against the germs that we greet peace as a definitely healthier people, organised to save, in a generation or two, for service in this world, more than the total of all those who went to a Higher Service from the fields of France and Belgium.

Because the war has given a sounder national discipline, because it has cleared so many obstacles from the path of medical organisation, the world's death-rate, according to sound calculations, will in future years show a substantial decrease. The toll taken by the Germans will be more than made up by the lives saved from the germs. The

THE MEDICAL SERVICES.

British Medical Service, following in the path of the victorious British Army, and wielding an authority that it never knew before, carried on a war against disease in Europe, Asia, and Africa that is now saving thousands of lives, and will save millions in the ultimate result. Enteric, cholera, dysentery, scurvy, small-pox, beri-beri, malaria, phthisis were fought successfully. Even that national British disease, rheumatism, was pushed back from some of its trenches and compelled to surrender not a few of its ridges.

Fascinating as a fairy tale, absorbing as a good detective story, stimulating as the records of a stubborn battle, will be the record of British medical work in the Great War when it comes to be written. It will not be a story merely of drains and drugs and dressings, but also of kindly amulets and beneficent golden fishes; of wicked germs who chalk their throats to deceive with soft talk little red corpuscles; of fairy princes who destroy wicked enchantments with spells from tiny glass tubes. Those attentive gentlemen experimenting with neck ribbons smeared with potent charms have not come to their second childhood; they are on the track of the perfectcimicifuge which will keep lice off the body and, keeping off lice, will reduce the range of typhus and other diseases. A great tank of little live fish sent out to a malaria Front does not mean that we are relapsing into the old Chinese school of medicine (which prescribed a live mouse to be swallowed whole as a remedy for one complaint), but that these little fish love to eat the eggs of the anopheles mosquito, which spreads malaria. It lays its eggs in ponds; the fish eat the eggs; the eggs don't hatch; the mosquitoes don't come; and there is less malaria.

If your mind is more attracted by detective stories than by fairy tales, turn to a bacteriological laboratory and watch the tracking down of the Hidden Hand that is responsible for odious diseases; for example, that one known popularly as spotted fever, a very deadly disease of over-crowding. A cunning criminal is the spotted fever germ, and he has not yet been quite fully identified and convicted. A victim of spotted fever has in his throat and spinal fluid the causative germ; but this germ hides behind a smoke cloud of other germs and must be placed quite definitely before it can be destroyed. It was found that it is a germ shaped like a double bean, that it is to be distinguished from other germs of the same shape by the fact that its hide is impervious to a certain stain which those other germs will absorb. It was further found that this spotted fever germ would not increase and multiply at a warmth of 23 degrees C., whilst otherwise similar germs would. There certain knowledge stopped for a time. Other double-bean, non-staining, non-growing at 23 degrees C. germs existed, among whom the real criminal lived and hid. Finally, four bad brother germs were found and are now being dealt with, and the disease is no longer a serious menace.

The divine purpose for good that runs stubbornly through life and has made it impossible for the murderous German plans to thrive in spite of all our neglects and stupidities, crops up insistently in the story of the British medical campaign in this war. Thus, chlorine gas came into the field first as the poison gas of the Germans; it remained in the field on the British side chiefly as a means for purifying water.

One interesting result of the war which we noticed at G.H.Q. was the abandonment of the Early Victorian primness in conversation in England. Soldiers going home on leave noticed it from 1916 onwards; and on the balance of the evidence I do not think they were at all responsible for it. They would go away from Boulogne, after an extra careful bath and the putting on of a clean tunic, with a steady resolution to put away from their thoughts and their tongues all the coarseness of the camp; and find themselves at their first dinner party in England tackled by some young lady in her teens on the subject of lice; or by some matron not yet in the thirties on the subject of venereal disease at the Front. They would come back often with a distinct feeling of shame-shock, to welcome the comparative reticence of Mess conversation.

It was my duty once to see the representative of an organisation that wished to have lectures delivered to all the soldiers on the subject of "v.d." To my surprise the representative proved to be a lady—and a young and attractive lady at that. She plunged into her subject without the least trace of embarrassment. She wanted lectures, with pictures, in every recreation hut of the B.E.F., France, and was firm to brush away the objection that "the men might not like it," and scornful of the reservation that if the lectures were permitted they were not to be "parade lectures," i.e., the men were not to be compelled to attend. Finally, discovering that though the lady wanted "pictures" she had not the pictures but expected the Army to supply them, I took refuge in a subterfuge. "Very sorry, very sorry indeed, but there is no Vote out of which we can get the pictures."

THE MUNITIONS OF THE WAR.

But the lady was insistent. She knew that there were cinematographs provided for the soldiers.

"Oh, but that is not my department. That is Amusements."

"Very well," she said firmly. "I'll see Amusements."

And she went away to convince some other Staff Officer that universal lectures on v.d., with pictures, would be an appreciated Amusement.

I do not know where the idea sprang from that v.d. was very common in the Army. So far as my observation went, and from what inquiries I made of medical officers, the opposite was the case. Among the officers with whom I came into touch during the campaign—many hundreds in the aggregate—I only heard of one case. Among the men of my battery before I was on the Staff I never heard of one case during 18 months of regimental life.

The Army's standard of health in this respect was better than that of the average of the civilian population. There were some tragic outbreaks—one in Cairo, another (of much less seriousness) with Amiens as its focus—but on an average the record was good.

British ideas did not favour the degrees of regulation and interference in this matter that other countries tolerate. But the soldier had some safeguards which the civilian had not. For instance it was the duty of the Assistant Provost Marshal of a Division, whenever a man reported sick from v.d., to go to the hospital, interview the patient and try to find out the *fons et origo*. If his mission were successful the person responsible was promptly expelled from the Army area.

One of the Dominion Corps adopted the method of advising prophylactic precautions (and supplying the means of prophylaxis). The British Army on a whole did not follow that course, though in the later stages of the campaign the means of prophylaxis were available if applied for.

But enough on that point. It was the surgical rather than the medical side of the R.A.M.C. that interested G.H.Q. So many had "taken a knock" and put in a spell at a hospital. Opinion was practically unanimous that "Hospital" was a place of real human sympathy as well as devoted skill, and that "sister" was the best pattern of womankind. It is etiquette in the Army to call her always "Sister," though technically "sister" is an intermediate grade between "nurse" and "matron." Matron is a great dignitary. She has, in the language of the Bar, "taken silk," and when her silk gown rustles into the room it is etiquette for officers to stand up, provided they have legs and strength to stand up. Otherwise you "come to attention" by smiling as well as you can; a respectful, cheerful, but not an hilarious or free-and-easy smile. It should convey the message that you are having the time of your life in the best possible of hospitals under the best possible of matrons. The Sister whose patient you are will be very much hurt if you do not smile properly at Matron. "Sister" is of many different grades of skill, but of an almost unvarying grade of devotion, the highest.

A "strafer," in hospital language, is a Sister who by ten years or so of hard anxious work and self-denial has reached to the height of an office boy's wage and a professional skill which saves lives daily and cuts weeks off one's stay in hospital. You are always glad when she has gone away from your wound, but at the back of your gladness is the knowledge that you want her for next dressing. A good "strafer" goes over a wound with the enthusiasm of a thrush with a large family going over a lawn for worms. She examines, searches, squeezes, probes, looking out for shed pieces of bone, for "proud flesh," for odd corners where inflammatory matter might lurk. She is looking for mischief, and any mischief found is promptly "strafed." If it is bad she calls in the doctor; if it is minor she has her own little armoury of mischief-breakers, scissors, pincers, nitrate of silver, and the like. Matrons are easily offended. At a certain hospital in France the King was half expected as a visitor. The Matron at once had a bad attack of decoration fever. As I was a lightly-wounded that time I assisted her policy of deceiving his Majesty into thinking that the hospital was always a fairy bower by going out and "finding" some flowers. Then Matron had clean quilts on all the beds, and the order went forth that these were to be kept creaseless and smooth. But one patient would persist in crooking up his knees. Matron argued with him. He disloyally pleaded that he was much more comfortable that way. Now, having got the flowers for the ward, I thought I had the right to give advice as a sort of accomplice, and I suggested mildly: "Better break his knees, Matron."

She was offended. Then the King did not come after all; and I think she was inclined to blame me for that.

But matrons are not altogether an evil; like the Staff and adjutants and brigade majors, they are at the worst necessary evils, at the best quite good sorts. But there is one matron-habit that should be dealt with sternly by regulation. If a very pretty nurse were posted to a hospital, Matron generally tried to assign her to the sick sisters' ward. Obviously that was bad strategy. The prettiness of their nurse would have no cheering effect on sick sisters, but to sick officers a pretty sister irresistibly suggests the wisdom of getting well quickly. Fortunately the supply of pretty sisters is too great to allow of their all being absorbed in wards for sick sisters.

A ROYAL VISIT, DECEMBER 1918

THE MUNITIONS OF THE WAR.

What reconciles one to Matron is the discovery sooner or later that, despite silk gown and awe-inspiring manner, she is at heart still "Sister," ready with skilful aid and encouraging sympathy in case of need. It is a nice etiquette that makes the title "Sister" general, for it is just sisterly affection which makes the atmosphere of a military hospital so cheering and recreating.

Distinctions of rank are abrogated in a military hospital to a large extent. The officer of general rank has a special quarter where he meets only other highnesses; but, for the rest, colonel and "pip-squeak" (the odious term which is vainly designed to lessen the self-importance of the second lieutenant) usually fraternise in a common cheerfulness. There are no rank badges on pyjamas. But one distinction has intruded—that between surgical cases and medical cases. The medical case must bear himself very humbly if he gets into a ward where there are surgical cases. Even that kindly authority "Sister" will in some unguarded moment, unless she is very, very careful, refer to him as *only* a medical case."

One medical case, taught cunning by circumstances, discovered when he was being moved from one hospital to another that a special sort of headache he suffered from could be relieved by a large, impressive bandage. With this head adornment he successfully deceived us at —— Hospital. A rumour went around that he was a trepanned case, and as Rumour stalked from bed to bed the size of the silver plate in his skull grew and grew until it was almost the size of a dinner plate. His shameful secret was at length discovered; he was only a fever or a heart or something, and, whilst we were all sorry for him, he no longer disputed favour with our ward pet—a delightfully cheerful pip-squeak whose body was so be-stitched that we felt sure they had a sewing machine in the operating room for him.

It is etiquette in a military hospital to be very much interested in one's neighbour's wounds and to affect to hold lightly one's own. It is very bad form to hint that your lot is more severe than his lot.

"Oh, I am all right, thanks," (you say in answer to his first advances); "except for a bit of my liver and a few yards of lung blown away, I'm as fit as can be. But that looks an awful leg of yours."

"Not at all, not at all. It is almost certain now to stay on. But it must be horribly interesting to have a body wound."

And so the ghoulish chat goes on.

Quite half of G.H.Q. had hospital reminiscences to exchange; indeed a spell in hospital with a bad wound was often the clinching argument leading to "red tabs" if an officer were qualified for the distinction; and Medical Boards in England were quite willing to certify a man as fit for France if he was marked for a Staff Appointment even though his category was "light duty."

"Trench Feet" gave the Medical Services more trouble than any other single disease, and almost as much trouble as the shells of the enemy. In the winter of 1915 a pilgrim to Flanders (supposing him to have a military permit) might have observed in the rest camps behind the British lines companies of men with bare feet, and officers bending down anointing them. And he might have perhaps concluded that this was some religious ritual of humiliation, such as the theatrical washing of beggars' feet by the late Austrian Emperor once a year. But such a conclusion would have been wrong. The proceeding was religious certainly, in the highest sense, but in no way theatrical. It was "Trench Feet" treatment.

The disease known as "Trench Feet" was one of the most serious developments which the Army on the Western Front had to face when the Germans, beaten in the field, "dug in," and Trench War began. The struggle with the disease was a long and strenuous one, taxing to the utmost the resources of the British Army Medical Service.

The causes of the disease were not plain at the outset, and inquiry proved them to be various. Everybody knows that it is uncomfortable and, to a certain extent, unhealthy to stand for too long at a time. (The social legislation that shop employees must be allowed seats is an indication of this). The soldier in the trenches must often stand for long periods. That makes him to some extent liable to foot trouble. Again, tight boots and tight bandages round the legs are bad for the blood circulation, and can make foot trouble without any other cause. The soldier used to be rather careless as to whether his boots were of a proper fit, and he was apt to bind his puttees too tightly.

Here were the beginnings of "Trench Feet." To have the feet wet, to have the feet cold for long spells, will cause chilblains, i.e., local inflammations showing first as red itching lumps, afterwards if neglected, developing into open sores. Long periods of standing, and any constriction of the circulation from tight boots or tight puttees, help cold and damp to cause chilblains; and chilblains used to be almost invariably neglected by the soldier. Then came the final aggravating cause—the filth of the Flanders mud getting into the sores of the broken chilblains, and, behold, a typical case of Trench Feet.

In the early days cases were often of dreadful severity, sometimes leading to amputation. In one of my billets at Montreuil was a French soldier who had lost both his feet from this cause. Later, both treatment of the disease and, more important, the prevention of it, were so perfected that really bad cases were rare.

The story of the fight against "Trench Feet" is one of the many fine stories of the war. In the main it was, of course, a story of medical skill and devotion, but also it was a story of unstinted generosity on the part of the War Office, and of admirable and intelligent service on the part of regimental officers. The medical staff told me that it would have been impossible to carry on to success the campaign against "Trench Feet" if they had not been intelligently and perseveringly backed up by regimental officers, and if the War Office had not poured out very many thousands of pounds sterling for the furtherance of every approved preventive measure.

Preventive measures covered a wide field; precautions against tight boots and tight puttees; increased provisions of socks; increased bathing facilities; provision of waterproof rubber boots for men while in the trenches (these boots were of the high wader type); paving of the trenches with "duck-boards" which gave a dry standing; more frequent reliefs in wet trenches. These were material provisions. To second them there was an active propaganda in personal hygiene, and here the regimental officer and non-commissioned officer were enlisted to help the medical staff to make the men understand that the smallest sign of a chilblain was to be met with prompt treatment. A whale oil ointment was provided both as a prophylactic and as a curative for mild chilblains. When necessary this was reinforced by spirituous lotions. On officers was put the responsibility of seeing that their men's feet were kept clean and well anointed with oil, and that any breach of the skin tissue was promptly treated. So officers became chiropodists, and you might see enthusiastic company commanders assisting their men to wash and anoint their feet, to show them how it should be done.

The winter of 1917-1918 put to a severe test the precautions against "Trench Feet," for in almost every part of the Western Front the British had pushed the Germans back, and there was no longer the old organised trench system. Nevertheless the British hospital records show that the disease was held. It was still a trouble; but, thanks to the plentiful supply of comforts and preventatives, and to the scrupulous care demanded by regimental and medical officers, it was no longer a grave menace.

The fight against mustard gas in 1918 was another fine achievement of the Medical Services. But this subject of the medicine of the war calls for a volume to itself. Let me only add here that the successful medical results won in this war were largely due to the fact that—contrary to the system of other wars—the doctor had a real influence and power at G.H.Q. In his own department he was supreme. So were solved successfully the vast medical problems which the Great War presented. The greatest armies known to history grappled in a continuous and furious struggle, not for a day or a night or a week, but for months. The wounds caused by hand grenades and high explosive shells were often of terrible extent. The battlefield to a depth of five miles was under constant shell fire, and transport of the wounded for that distance was therefore always under fire, and roads were torn up almost as soon as made. Conditions of infection were extraordinarily favourable. Traffic regulation had to overcome the most serious obstacles, since railways, roads and tracks had to provide for the constant reinforcements, for the frequent passage to and fro of relieving Divisions, for food and water for men and horses, and also for ammunition unprecedented in quantity.

CHAPTER VII.

THE ANIMALS OF THE FORCE.

A happy lot—The mud season in Flanders—The effects of mustard gas—The character of the mule—Forage difficulties—The French object to our horse ration—The Americans side with us—The animal record in 1918.

No two officials at G.H.Q. had a better right to be proud of their departments than the Director of Veterinary Services (Major-General Moore) and the Director of Remounts (Brigadier-General Sir F. S. Garratt). These two were responsible for the welfare of the half million animals of the B.E.F., and there was never a collection of war animals that had a better time.

It was a commonplace of German criticism of Great Britain's military position before 1914 that the possibilities of a big quickly-trained British Army were negligible, because, whilst rank and file might be raised quickly enough, three things could not be improvised in a hurry: knowledge of staff work, of gunnery, and of horse-mastery. The German now knows that he was wrong, and in no particular was he more wrong than in regard to horse-mastery. It is admitted over all the Continent of Europe that horse-mastery in the "improvised" British Army reached the highest standard of the campaign.

In this matter the horse markets of Europe spoke after the Armistice with no uncertain voice. When the British Army was disposing of its superfluous horses, everybody rushed to buy them. Prices touched a truly extraordinary level. The unhappy taxpayer amid all his burdens saw a golden stream flowing into the Treasury, because his Army was a humane, conscientious, and skilful horsemaster. The military advantage to transport through keeping the Army's animals fit and well is so obvious that it need not be dwelt upon. The advantage to the *morale* of the men is not so generally appreciated, but was none the less real. It helped to keep our men in good heart that the animals who worked with them, and for them, were in good heart and condition. To British men with their fine tradition of humanity to animals it would have been demoralising to have seen their brutes hungry and suffering. Finally, the world markets came forward with their evidence that the British Army policy of kindness to its animals was not only good for transport and good for *morale* but also good for business.

By the Spring of 1919 we had sold out of the Army 252,676 animals (horses and mules), of which 235,715 were sold for work and 16,961 for meat. The total realised was £8,493,920, of which £8,081,607 was realised from the working animals and £412,313 for those animals which, because of old age or disablement, it was more merciful to send to the slaughter-house. In addition a small item of £18,696 had been realised from by-products, for our Army administrators, whatever might be thought to the contrary, did study economy, and the animal which fell by the wayside was usually put to some use. At least its hide was saved, and, if transport were available, its fat and bones also figured in a "salvage" return.

This money was mostly foreign money, too. It was the policy of the Army not to "profiteer" in the United Kingdom. Indeed, within our home borders it was rather to help the small farmer with cheap animals than to seek to get the best out of the market.

The mobilisation of the horse strength of Great Britain in 1914 was wonderfully assisted by the willing and instructed patriotism of farmers, landowners, and hunting men. It yielded far better results than were anticipated. One calculation makes it that 17 per cent. of the total civilian horse strength of the country was mobilised.

But, of course, there was a tremendous gap between this result and the needs of the New Armies. A wise prescience at the very outset decided to reinforce horse strength with mule strength. Before the end of 1914 mules imported from abroad were being tried as substitutes for horses in the Army. Some of the experiments did not give promising results. The mule, for example, did not prove possible in gun teams. But it established itself in a very wide range of general utility and materially helped to win the war.

The improvisation of remount depôts and of training centres for horses and for men who for the first time had to handle horses was the first big problem. The winter of 1914-15 was a hard time. But extraordinary results were won by the cordial co-operation of the "horsey" men of the country. The hunting, coaching, and racing

THE ANIMALS OF THE FORCE.

stables were great pillars of strength. By the spring of 1915 the position in the United Kingdom was good.

In the winter of 1915-16 most of the difficulty had to be faced by the B.E.F., France. We had a great concentration of troops in Flanders. The mounted units were made up in the main of men new to horse-management. The animals had to be nursed through a winter in what was the wickedest country conceivable for horses. Stable accommodation was, of course, absent. Not 1 per cent. could be housed in existing stables. Labour and material were lacking for the building of new stables. Most of the animals spent the winter in the open. The mud was a cruel enemy. In that highly manured country a horse standing out in the mud had its hoofs attacked at once. A "greasy heel" soon became a purulent sore.

The "Mud Season" opens in Flanders in October and lasts until June; and Flanders mud has a body and aroma all its own. A great French Marshal of a by-gone age committed himself without reserve to the opinion that "Flanders was no place to fight in." Thomas Atkins, as he pushed obstinately and irresistibly through the mud towards some pill-box objective, has endorsed that high strategical judgment. Perhaps in a future war, if there is going to be a future war, Flanders will be a closed area and no Army will be allowed to go there to fight under penalty of a *procès-verbal*. That should be done if only for the sake of the horses.

THE EAST RAMPARTS

THE ANIMALS OF THE FORCE.

As every civilian stay-at-home knows, the Army is an entirely foolish organisation with no knowledge of practical affairs. But I doubt whether any civil organisation would have carried the same number of horses through the same conditions with the same small percentage of losses. The Army did not tackle the problem in any hide-bound way. A good deal was left to the initiative and enthusiasm of individual officers. Some general principles were set down. Within the boundaries of those principles there was wide scope for personal ingenuity, and as the good thing that one officer worked out soon became the property of all the Division, a very high standard of horse-management was reached.

Will it shock some old retired officers to hear that authority, the highest authority, abolished the clipping of horses that year in Flanders? Horse-clipping was once a sacred institution, with its fixed dates and ritual, in the Army.

That year in Flanders horse-clipping was abolished, and the horses became wild and woolly but withal happy. I used to love to see their flowing locks streaming in the cold wind as they stood out in the lines, coated like St. Bernard dogs, and quite comfortable. "Stables" became more arduous as horse-coats became longer, but the horses flourished in the open with just break-winds, and sometimes thatch rain-shelter overhead. I would never want to see a finer lot of horses than those of the early Spring of 1916. They were hairy and they were lean, and they would eat their nosebags, if given a minute's grace after the feed was finished; but they were full of heart and of work.

The enemy was the mud. We found that if the horses were given good standings and their feet kept out of the mud the rain did not trouble them at all, and the wind troubled them little. But once off the pavé roads all Flanders was semi-liquid, and the problem at horse-lines was first to secure a solid "standing," next to secure a solid road in and out to that standing, and finally to secure a solid road to and from a solid watering place. A unit that built for its horses elegant brick standings in the middle of a field, and forgot the rest, found after the first rain that its lines were surrounded by a sea of mud. Then the horses had to be given temporary refuge in the paved street of an evacuated town, whilst a saddened unit faced scorn and obloquy and the necessity of constructing another brick standing on another site, *not* an island site this time.

Standings were usually made of bricks, and the Army requisitioned all the brick yards in the occupied area. Shell-ruined villages were another source of brick supply. Rubble brick was of no use for standings; the bricks had to be set properly; rubble was lost in the soil within a day. One officer got excellent results by preparing a well-sloped bed; enclosing it with great logs, treating it with a thin layer of straw, and close-setting the bricks over that. It seemed a poor use to put straw to, but that stand lasted out the winter wonderfully well.

The difficulty of getting good accessible watering places was very great. Water, of course, there was in abundance, but the horses would ordinarily have to go up to their bellies in mud to get at it. To set up troughs accessible by some firm road was necessary, and the site of the troughs had to be soundly paved. One Pioneer officer settled his watering problem ingeniously. He had secured a pump and some hose, and he sank a little well just on the edge of his horse-lines, and was able to water by troughs set up on the brick standing. Watering by bucket was forbidden except on the road, for the reason that there was never any certainty by bucket watering that a horse would get enough to drink, and a horse kept short of water for long is soon a lost horse.

Losses from enemy action were not very high among the horses until the last phase. There was, on the whole, little cavalry work except at the end of the campaign and at its very beginning. Our air supremacy usually saved horse-lines in the rear of our lines from very severe shelling. But horse and mule losses increased greatly when the enemy began to use mustard gas. That proved deadly to animals. The ground where a mustard gas shell had fallen was infected for many hours afterwards. If horses were picketed on it, or even passed over it, casualties were high. The irritant poison of the gas attacked their skins wherever the hair was thin, and caused the most dreadful wounds. Precaution, however, was prompt, and an effective curative treatment was found in a dressing, the chief ingredient of which was chloride of lime.

From the spring of 1918 the British Army horse had to suffer severe attacks from the air. We had by then established a very great transport superiority, and the enemy devoted a good deal of his air strength to bombing attacks on our horse-lines, with a view to lessening our transport strength. At first these attacks were very deadly. But the position was soon met. Horse-lines were cleverly concealed. The animals were separated into small groups. The lines were protected by bomb-proof traverses of earthwork, which localised the effects of explosions.

THE ANIMALS OF THE FORCE.

In the summer of 1918 the wastage of animals had been cut down to the lowest percentage reached in the whole campaign. This meant that battle losses were being compensated for by a very low sickness rate, achieved by careful and skilful horse-mastership. The British Army, which had been always an army of horse-lovers, was now also an Army of skilled horse-masters, and in spite of bombing raids, of long-distance shelling, and of poison gas, the death rate kept dwindling. At this time forage difficulties were acute, but there had been close organisation to grow fodder in Army and Line of Communication areas, and our animals always had a decent ration.

But it was through the unsparing work of the men, with brain and hand, that the horses were so happily situated. The public at Home can never express sufficient gratitude for that work—work which had little glamour or hope of reward, but which was as necessary to victory as that of rifleman and gunner.

The final triumph of our Army horse administration was in the summer of 1918, when it was able to take up a big part of the burden of horsing the American units arriving in France. That, again, was a factor of victory. Without transport or gun-horses the American troops could not have given their magnificent help in the last stages of the campaign.

In the sum the story of the British Army horse in the Great War is a thrilling one. Our Home horse-lovers opened the chapter gloriously. The British Navy followed up by making it possible to transport remounts from all parts of the world. Then the men of the Old Army and of the New Armies showed what grit and resource and kindness could do. So we rode home to victory.

The record of the animals of the B.E.F. should do something to dissipate the marked prejudice against the mule in Great Britain. People here do not understand its virtues as a draught animal. Granted that the mule is not suitable for heavy draught work and may prove a serious nuisance on a farm if it cannot be kept within its proper bounds—for a mule has an omnivorous appetite—still there is a very wide field of usefulness for this animal in city work, such as bread and milk and parcel carriage and light van work generally; also as a transport animal for the small farmer. The mule eats much less than the horse, has a longer working life, is less liable to disease, needs less attention. The mule's rough commonsense, which teaches him to be very careful of himself, is a positive advantage. Given decent treatment, a mule is a reliable, good-natured, and likeable animal. He has not the same charming manners as a well-trained horse, but he has plenty of character, and it is mostly good character.

The wicked mule does exist, but he is the exception, not the rule. One champion wicked mule I can recall. He was as big as a horse, black in colour, and on the near side had a blood-shot fiery eye which was a good danger signal. On the off-side he had a white eye. This was a deceptive white-flag signal, for the beast kicked with equal viciousness on both sides. Likewise he bit from all points of the compass. The one thing that soured his life was the fact that he couldn't sting with his tail. To groom Belial—that was his name—he had to be put in slings. But he was an easy animal to shoe. Hold a shoe with the nails fixed in the proper position, and the animal would attach itself firmly to the shoe with one kick. An occasional Belial excepted, the mules were a pleasant lot.

The mule is a hard worker but a sensible worker. He will not try to overtax his strength, and he goes on strike firmly if asked to do too much. "I may be a bit of an ass," the animal tells you, "but none of this heroic business of the Arab steed breaking his heart with a mighty effort for *me*."

This attitude is not poetic, but it is practical. And the mule compensates by standing mud better, eating less, and putting up with poorer food than the horse. The mule, however, is very particular about what he drinks. Water that the horse will swallow greedily the mule will turn up his Roman nose at. If you are watering mules and horses at the same stream, the mules must have first drink, for they will not touch the muddied water, though horses have no objection to it.

G.H.Q. during the last stages of the campaign had a hard task to keep the animals of the B.E.F. properly fed. At the outset of the War the horse ration erred, if anything, on the generous side, and a good deal of it wandered into the mangers of the civilian animals of the country, much to their contentment. As the war dragged its exhausting length along, money became scarce, food supplies scarcer still, and transport facilities scarcest of all. Then the ration of the animals had to be cut to a point which represented just sufficient and nothing more. Even so, it was a much better ration than the French gave their horses, and there were repeated efforts by the French Authorities to persuade us to come down to their animal ration. Those efforts naturally had a much greater chance of success when the union of the command made Marshal Foch the Generalissimo of all the Armies in France.

THE ANIMALS OF THE FORCE.

But our High Command was stubborn in its championship of the animals. There was a very strong representation of the cavalry on the Staff; and, besides, the British as a race have a sentiment about animals which is not shared to the full by the Latin races. The average British soldier would as soon go short of food himself as see his animals hungry. At one time the British War Cabinet yielded to the strong representations that were being made that the British Army wasted resources and transport in its feeding of the animals, and ordered a heavy reduction of the horse ration. Even then the British Command in the Field did not give up the cause for lost, continued to argue the matter, and by pointing out that a vast amount of extra work was just then being thrown upon the animals by the reduction of Field Artillery ammunition teams from six horses to four, secured a compromise decision which made a much smaller reduction in the ration.

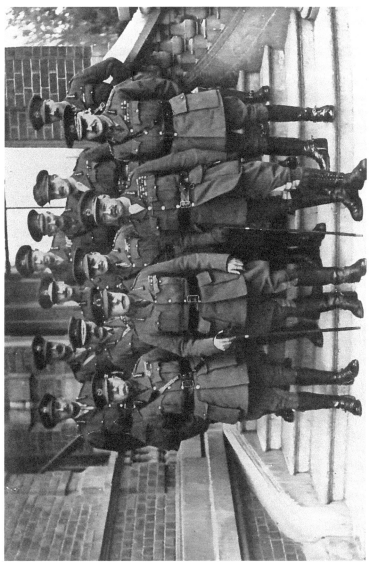

THE ARMY COMMANDERS

THE ANIMALS OF THE FORCE.

The French Authorities without a doubt honestly believed they were in the right and that we were "coddling" our brutes, for they made another effort to get "unity of animal ration" as a kind of logical sequel to "unity of command." This time they made an agreement with the Americans that the latter should come down to their scale of animal ration. Without a full knowledge of what they were doing, the Americans agreed at first; and it looked as if the British horse also would have to have his ration reduced. But with more complete knowledge of the facts the American Army reversed its previous decision and decided that it could not come down below the British animal ration. A whinny of joy would have gone round the British horse lines at this decision if it had been promulgated in horse language, for it saved the situation. I am honestly of opinion that it had its effect, too, in bringing the campaign to its triumphant conclusion. In the last stages between August and November, 1918, I do not think that the rapid pursuit of the enemy would have been possible if the horse ration had been reduced further than it was in July, 1918. As it was, that reduction put a stop to the decline in the sickness rate and caused it to increase slightly.

G.H.Q. did its best to make up for the reduced ration by organising local growth of fodder crops wherever there was a chance, and there was instituted an Inspectorate of Horse Feeding and Economies. The I.Q.M.G.S. had to oversee all animals, except those on charge of Director Remounts and Director Veterinary Services, to advise on all matters of forage, to seek means of economy and generally to supervise the "horse-mastery" of units.

Horse-masters can best judge the rights of the fodder position for themselves by noting the actual animal ration. Taking an average of 25,000 horses, light *and* heavy, the weight of the rations at the time of the controversy was:

	lbs.
American	23.6
British	22.2
French	16.1

Twenty-two pounds weight of food per day is not excessive for a horse doing hard work; and that was the *average*. After the heavy horses had their higher ration the light horses had to be content with less.

Probably the French never saw our point of view and suspected that there was not much more than English obstinacy in this determined stand for the welfare of the dumb beasts. But the controversy was carried on with good humour all the same, and in the end "those curious English" had their own way.

Whenever questions such as this arose between the Allied Forces it proved in practice that the Americans usually had the deciding voice. Perhaps it may be recorded without hurting anyone's feelings that the American as a matter of instinct was inclined usually to take the French side, because his stronger sympathy was in that direction; after experience he was inclined usually to take the British side, for his manner of thinking was more on our lines.

The animal record for the last year of the war was a fine one. The sickness rate was brought down to a figure practically as low as that of a big stable under peace conditions, and this—the result of good horse-mastery—helped to make up for battle casualties and casualties from bombs. (It was in January, 1918, that the enemy first instituted a definite policy of searching out our horse-lines and subjecting them to aeroplane attack in order to cripple our lines of supply). In June, 1918, the sickness rate was actually lower than at any period in the history of the force (7.7 per cent. as against 12.05 per cent. in May, 1917). Losses of animals in battle showed a marked reduction. The general reduction in losses was partly due to a decrease in the losses from enemy bombs, as a great deal of work had then been done to conceal and protect horse-lines from aircraft attack.

In July, 1918, the horse situation was even better, and the sickness rate for the month was 7.5 per cent. (compared with 7.7 per cent. in June and 8.73 per cent. in May). Unfortunately it was necessary that month to reduce the hay ration by one lb. per day. (A more considerable reduction proposed was abandoned, as I have pointed out). The shortage in the supply of animals as compared with requirements, a shortage principally due to the needs of the new American units, was met by various expedients. Nearly 25,000 animals were made available by reductions of the horse strength of artillery units. A further 14,000 were saved by giving 6-inch howitzer and some 60-pounder batteries mechanical transport. Another means of economy in horse-flesh was worked out—the setting up of a "Category B" in animals. Those which were not quite fit for arduous work with a fighting unit were withdrawn to units whose demands on them were less exacting.

In August, 1918, when our great attack began, the animals with the Force had heavy losses. Battle casualties were high, partly because of the large employment of cavalry, partly because of the intensive war from the air against horse-lines. The precautions against this kind of attack which we had developed could not be kept up during the rapid advance, and horses in the fighting line suffered severely from bombs as well as shell fire. But that was part of the necessary price of victory. What was a matter for real regret, however, was the increase in the sick rate which accompanied the revival of intensive operations. We all felt sorry that the forage ration had been reduced, even though slightly, for there was reason to think that even this slight reduction in the forage ration had made it impossible in some cases to keep the animals up to the best standard of condition. Very hard work was being done on a ration which was cut very fine.

After November 11th, when the Armistice was signed, our animal sickness rate was only 9 per cent., and later, as we began to sell off our animals, the advantage of humane treatment told in the market rates.

CHAPTER VIII.

THE FINANCIAL SERVICES.

The generosity of the British People—G.H.Q. was not a spendthrift—The Pay system—Curiosities of banking in the field—Claims of the civilian inhabitants—The looted rabbit.

THE financial side of the B.E.F. was one of the triumphs of G.H.Q. "Yes, in spending money," someone may remark, thinking gloomily over his Income Tax assessment. But the triumph I refer to is in the dealing with vast sums with so little loss from peculation or from mistake.

An Army in the Field should not be pinched for money if it is to work with confidence and economy of life. Very often in the history of war a "ragged Army" has done wonders, and the praise of those wonders has led to some minds confusing raggedness with heroism, thinking that desperate impoverishment is a good thing for an Army. It might have been sometimes in the old days, when the sack of the enemy's country was the reward of victory and it was a case of fight or perish. In modern times it is a sound principle of warfare that the better an Army is supplied with the means of warfare the less will be the cost of life in achieving its purpose.

The soldiers of the British Army in France have reason to feel grateful to the people of Great Britain that there was never any sparing of money at the expense of their comfort and safety. No Army at any known period of the world's history was more lavishly provided for in food, clothing, munitions and pay. To illustrate on one point only, that of munitions. In the British Army 100,000 men in a day used 410 tons of munitions, in the French Army the same number of men in a day used 246 tons. Part of the disparity might be accounted for by superior economy on the part of the French. Most of it was due to the fact that the British people were able to supply, and did supply, their troops with far greater quantities of shell, etc., so as to take as much of the burden of war as possible off the flesh and blood of the soldier.

THE FINANCIAL SERVICES.

The taxpayer for his part can be comforted with the knowledge that, so far as the Army in the Field was concerned, there was an honest effort to guard against waste. Of course war is a wasteful business, essentially, and no possible precaution can guard against some losses. Often the position is that a great amount of material has to be devoted to a certain purpose though it is very likely to be wasted, because the alternative is to incur a greater risk of life. It was always the British system, a system which Parliament insisted upon equally with the Generals in the Field, that any sacrifice of money and material was to be preferred to a useless sacrifice of life.

In peace times the Finance Branch of the War Office had a long-standing reputation for artful meanness. It was accused of working on the principle that an officer in the Army was always possessed of abundant private means and therefore never really wanted any Army money, and that a private soldier was clearly a fool and a failure for being in the Army at all and therefore deserved little or no consideration. If he were allowed money to spare he would waste it on dissipation.

Certainly F. Branch War Office showed itself time and again very sharp at construing the Pay Warrant to the benefit of the Treasury, but it was never quite as bad as that. In the Field the spirit of economy had to give place to the spirit of efficiency and of *morale*. Nevertheless, a very tight check was kept on the money-bags to prevent dishonesty or extravagance. The Financial Adviser at G.H.Q. was a potentate of great ability and of enormous authority. No order which involved the spending of money could go out without being referred to him and winning his approval. He had the right of access to the Commander-in-Chief at all times. It was said that since as a civilian he did not get prompt and full respect from sentries, or from officers who did not understand his position as Chancellor of the Army Exchequer, he was made a General in a single day, and that when he first walked abroad as a General and sentries presented arms to him he was greatly perturbed, thinking that this might be the first step in an outbreak of personal violence. But that was by way of *persiflage*. All officers who came into contact with him recognised a man of ability and of sympathy.

It was the Army Pay Department that most closely touched the lives of the soldiers in France. It had to pay a total of about two and a half million people of all kinds—officers who were either affluent or careful and gave no trouble at all; officers who were neither and whose impecuniosity had to be guarded against; a very few officers who were actually dishonest; "other ranks" in whose pay there were infinite complications due to separation allowances and the like; and furthermore the women of the various auxiliary corps, the Labour Corps of various nationalities, civilian auxiliaries and the like. As the war progressed "Pay" had to act as money changer, dealing with almost all the currencies of the world, and as a Savings Bank and as liquidator of all kinds of claims and as a third party in those highly convenient transactions in which an officer bought clothes and other necessities from "Ordnance" at a price which was sometimes less than half that charged by London stores.

The Army Pay Department in the Field was not the final paymaster. It gave advances on account only, leaving the final adjustment to the Pay office at Home. But during the war and up to the end of 1918 (by which time demobilisation had broken up most of the units in France) it had paid out nearly four thousand million francs, and its total losses from forgeries, war losses, bad money, etc., were quite insignificant. At one period in 1918 when an analysis was made, it was found that the bad money passed off on to the Pay Department had averaged only eight francs per week.

The financial arrangements of the old Regular Army had to be modified very considerably, especially in regard to officers, as the war continued, though at first an attempt was made to apply them in their entirety. The Army Pay Agents soon found out that a number of the new officers who had come into the service had little or no sense of financial responsibility, and the Pay Department had to tighten the reins considerably. Exceedingly liberal arrangements had been made at the outset to meet the convenience of officers. Thus any Branch of the Bank of France would cash an officer's cheque up to £5, and any Field Cashier—each Division had a Field Cashier—would cash his chit to the same amount. Also, he might draw his allowances by cheque monthly, and this cheque was good at any Field Cashier's office.

Some early developments were startling. There is a tale of one officer (he was in a position which gave him a wide range of movement) collecting £125 in one day before going on leave. He had a "good leave" presumably, but he had at the time only £3 due to him at his Army Agent's, and it took some time for him to make up the balance on his pay as lieutenant. To meet the case of gentlemen "raising the wind" on this scale there was instituted an "Officer's Advance Book," the conditions of obtaining and using which were gradually tightened, so that it was only possible for an officer below "field" rank to obtain three advances in a month of 125 francs each. That still left one loop-hole for improvidence or dishonesty—cashing cheques at a Bank of France after drawing the three advances. But not very many officers could get to a bank except during a "leave," and a certain "overrunning of the constable" was expected then and could be adjusted afterwards. Officers who consistently drew beyond their means after warning were looked upon as having dishonest intentions and were put on a "black list." They could not draw cheques, and were deprived of their "Advance Books" until they were in credit again.

There was no serious amount of financial delinquency. At the worst the "black list" just crept over the 100 limit. One incorrigible spendthrift, having been deprived of his Advance Book, tried to obtain another from a Field Cashier in another centre on the plea that his previous book "had been captured by the enemy."

It was very human, the Pay Department, for all its strictness, and in my experience never refused an officer who was going on leave a "bit extra" if he had a good financial name. One of its very kind customs was to arrange for wounded officers evacuated to "Blighty" to be met in England by Pay Agents who pressed on them change of a little cheque to meet possible incidental expenses in hospital. It had, too, a nice habit of watching the tactical situation and acting accordingly. After the great German onrush of the Spring of 1918 many hundreds of officers were destitute, their kits abandoned to the enemy. Pay Department promptly relaxed all its rules to enable them to outfit again promptly; and, of course, there was ultimately reimbursement to the officers of the value of their kits. Up to the conclusion of the war "Pay" reimbursed nearly 20,000 officers for loss of kit.

Photo by J Russell & Sons
MAJOR-GENERAL SIR CLAUDE A. BRAY
(Paymaster-in-chief, B.E.F.)

THE FINANCIAL SERVICES.

"Pay" changed any sort of money into French currency; and it had to deal with many varieties. Serbian, Egyptian, Nova Scotian, Greek, Kruger money (from South Africa), Australian bank notes, Italian, Russian, American, Canadian, local French "Bank of Commerce" notes (which were monetised in some cases by the Bank of France), Mexican dollars—all came to its counter and were duly honoured. But it turned up its nose at American Confederate Bank notes and assignats of the First French Republic (both useless except for wall paper).

Various currency problems had to be solved by "Pay." The Bank of France was always in a state of worry over the huge consumption of 5 francs notes by the British Army. These were the most favoured units for paying the men; they seemed to disappear from currency at a quick rate, and they were expensive to print. The situation was improved by the adoption of the suggestion of "Pay" that a 10-francs note should be issued. Probably the Bank of France would have been quite content if they had thought that the 5 francs notes were destroyed. But they knew that they were being hoarded up by the French peasants, who absorbed every bit of silver as soon as it was put into circulation, and, after silver, favoured for their hoards notes of small denominations. At the time of the German advance in the Spring of 1918 "Pay" had a curious illustration of the hoarding ways of these French peasants. That advance let loose a flood of silver coinage. The people who lived in districts which might have to be evacuated changed their hoarded silver for notes, which would be more handy to carry away.

"Pay" at an early stage of the war put forward an interesting proposal—the issue of International Army Notes in various denominations which would be good in any one of the Allied Countries. The proposal was never carried through, but its idea is being revived in the financial world to-day by the proposal for an International Bank to take over some or all of the war debts of the Allies and issue a paper currency good in any one of the Allied Countries.

The encouragement of thrift among the soldiers was part of the work of "Pay." In August, 1915, it secured soldier subscriptions to the War Loan to the extent of £25,200. The next year it established Savings Banks, and in 1918 it set up agencies at all Army Post Offices for the sale of War Savings Certificates. But its greatest achievement in the way of thrift was the Chinese Savings Bank, which was started in August, 1918, and in a fortnight had deposits of 400,000 francs.

G. H. Q. (MONTREUIL-SUR-MER)

The last welcome task of "Pay" was to establish Field Cashiers in Germany and to fix a rate of exchange for German money, which was started at five marks=2s. 8d.

The Claims Commission (established in December, 1914) was another branch of the financial organisation. Its business was to decide upon claims for damage done by the British Army to the property of civilians, French or Belgian. The British Army paid for everything, even to an orchard tree that an Army mule had nibbled at. Claims made were sometimes ridiculous in character and in extent. In my regimental experience I remember a market gardener claiming 200 francs on account of damage done by a horse which had wandered into his potato patch for a few minutes. The claim was very amicably settled on the spot by the payment in cash of two francs. On an average, "Claims" paid about one fourth of the total asked for, and the civilian population did very well indeed on that.

In the very early days of the war the civil population of France, filled with relief and gratitude at the arrival of the British Force, of whose coming they had almost despaired, greeted officer and soldier with the most generous hospitality. Indeed as the "Old Contemptibles" marched through Boulogne women stripped off their rings to give them to the marching soldiers. Wine, fruit, and other delicacies were pressed on everybody without payment. That generous enthusiasm could not last through a four years' war, but to the very end the best of the French population recognised a duty of hospitality to their British guests. It was only natural, however, that many of the peasants and small traders, hard hit by the war, should take advantage of their opportunities to make profit out of our Army. This was particularly noticeable after the coming of the Colonial troops, who were just as lavish in spirit as the British Tommies and had a good deal more pay to spend.

MAJOR-GENERAL L. B. FRIEND
(President of Claims Commission)

G. H. Q. (MONTREUIL-SUR-MER)

The Claims Commission, which in the later stages of the war had its headquarters at Paris Plage and Le Touquet, did its work to the satisfaction of everybody. At first its responsibilities were confined to paying claims for damage done. Later it took over all the financial adjustments in connection with the hiring and the requisition of civilian land and property. Its tasks called for a great deal of tact and a wide variety of resourcefulness. In the Spring of 1918 the abandonment in evacuated areas by civilians of wine and portable property caused trouble. The events at Amiens illustrate the position. As soon as the city came under enemy shell fire the civil authorities left, and with them most of the respectable inhabitants. Less respectable people remained, and probably were guilty of some excesses. The British Army Authorities, however, were prompt in taking over control, and on April 3rd the city was quiet and orderly. But very serious reports of damage by British troops were put into circulation. On investigation by the Claims Department the actual cases resolved themselves into two: in one house three doors had been broken down; in the other case the British Army had stolen a rabbit "which had been abandoned by its owners." These were the only two charges definitely preferred. But it was, seemingly, a fact that in some villages outside of Amiens regrettable incidents arose from the fleeing civilians abandoning stores of wine or disposing of them to the troops at sacrifice prices. The French Authorities were asked to assist in forbidding the importation by civilians of intoxicants into threatened areas.

Towards the end of the war some of the French towns which had been sheltering large numbers of British troops raised the question of the payment of octroi duties on the goods consumed by the troops. As I suppose is well known, French towns have local customs duties (called octroi because the right to collect them for local purposes was originally a concession from the King). All food, etc., coming into the town pays a small tax. Supplies for the British Army did not pay this tax, and the towns complained of the loss thus caused to their municipal revenues. G.H.Q. willingly conceded the payment of octroi. A lump sum was allowed for the past period, and an arrangement made for the future payment of so much per head every half year for each soldier billetted within the town boundaries. The *per capita* charge varied greatly. A few French towns refused to make any claim, saying that they were well content to make that concession to their British guests.

THE FINANCIAL SERVICES.

On the whole the financial record of the British Army in France is something to be proud of. We paid justly—sometimes generously—for everything, and no civilian was left with a legitimate grievance.

CHAPTER IX.

THE ECONOMY SERVICES.

What the German submarines taught us—The Salvage Organisation—O.C. Rags, Bones and Swill—Agriculture's good work and hard luck—The Forestry Directorate— Soldiers learn economy in a stern school.

THERE is a sort of grim pleasantry in the fact that the German submarine war, which was to bring Great Britain to her knees, only brought her to a school of economy where she learned some lessons which will be very useful in the future, once the after-the-war phase of reckless extravagance has passed away. When the cumulative effect of the unlimited submarine war made itself felt in 1918 it did not stop operations, though it may claim some of the responsibility for the extent of the German success in the Spring of that year, which might have been much more limited if we had had full supplies of wire and other defence material. What it did do was to set G.H.Q. to devising valuable economies.

The German was in effect too late with this, as with his other desperate steps. At the outset of the war, with an inferior sea power, Germany had yet the chance of using sea forces with great, and perhaps decisive, effect by raids on the British supply routes with light cruisers and converted merchantmen. She had prepared for this but neglected the one necessary act of forethought and daring by not sending out to sea her commerce destroyers. Such a sea policy would, of course, have been ruthless; but it could have been made effective without violation of sea law and without outrages on neutrals. After August, 1914, Germany sought vainly to repair her initial lack of sound naval sense by the submarine naval war, in which every canon of sea law and every sentiment of justice and humanity were violated. The more the submarine war showed signs of failing the more atrocious and reckless it became, until in its final shape it set almost all the world against the German Empire. Yet withal the U-boat atrocities went for nothing. The German people must see now that their Prussian masters put them very much in the position of the innkeeper of the old creepy German story. He and his wife resolved to kill in his sleep and rob a chance traveller who had come to their inn. They killed him and found that his purse was empty and that he was their own long-lost son.

On the debit side, as a result of the German submarine war we had in 1918 a lack of certain material—particularly of chocolate, biscuits, and tinned fruits in the canteens. On the credit side we had those fine economy organisations, Salvage, Agriculture and Forestry, the effect of which was not only to make savings at the time but also to teach the soldier a fuller appreciation of his civil duties.

"Salvage" explained itself very clearly in its official publication: "The world shortage of almost every kind of raw material used for war supplies makes Salvage an important Administrative Service. Without a well-organised and thorough Salvage system, the full maintenance of our Force in the Field would be made difficult.

"The co-ordination of all Salvage work is in the hands of the Controller of Salvage at G.H.Q. His duties include the inspection of executive Salvage work, the arrangements for the disposal of Salvage material, the investigation of methods for recovering bye-products, and keeping of statistical records showing the amount of material salved and disposed of and the resultant gain to the State.

"The Salvage Organisation is not intended to take the place of, or in any way discourage, a consistent effort on the part of every supply department to recover for repair and re-issue its own articles and its own empties. It is intended to supplement that effort; to collect and put to use what would otherwise become derelict; to ensure that nothing utilisable is allowed to go to waste.

"To this end it is necessary to arrange, in the first place, for the collection of unserviceable or derelict material, and, in the second, for its disposal so that it may be brought again into use with the least delay and to the best advantage."

AN ARMY POSTER

THE ECONOMY SERVICES.

"Salvage," in order to secure a practical interest in its work, used to issue statements to the soldiers showing how salved articles were utilised. Some examples:

Clothing:	Cleaned and repaired locally. If beyond repair, sent to the United Kingdom as rags.
Sacking:	Sent to the United Kingdom.
Entrenching tools:	Heads cleaned and sharpened. If irreparable, dis posed of as scrap.
Steel helmets:	Cleaned and relined. If irreparable, indiarubber pads in lining removed and utilised for lining serviceable helmets. Chin strap sold as old leather, and helmet disposed of as scrap steel.
Rubber gum boots, tyres, etc.):	Sent to Paris for classification and repair. If irreparable, sent to the United Kingdom. Cleaned in caustic soda, reblocked, resoldered if necessary, and retinned. If irreparable, disposed of as scrap steel.
Mess tins, camp kettles, field kitchen boilers:	Old felt removed—bottles cleaned, recovered with new felt and recorked. Old felt sent to the United Kingdom.
Water-bottles:	Water-bottles not fit for re-issue as such are used for packing small quantities of oil or paint for the Front.
Web equipment, cotton bandoliers, etc.:	Broken into component parts—dry-cleaned on motor-driven brushes, darned and repaired. If irreparable, sent to the United Kingdom as cotton rags, after brass or metal fittings have been removed.
Leather equipment, harness, saddlery, etc.:	Broken down into component parts, washed with soft soap in lukewarm water, dried in a drying cupboard at 100 deg. F., treated with fish-oil and repaired. If irreparable, sent to United Kingdom as old leather after brass or metal fittings have been removed.
Boots:	Classified, repaired and passed through fish-oil baths. The uppers of irreparable boots as far as possible made into shoe laces or heel lifts and used for filling.

G. H. Q. (MONTREUIL-SUR-MER)

"Salvage" had to suffer much from kindly "ragging." It was known as "Rags and Bones," and as "Swill." It was the favoured sport of the humourist to devise new salvage dodges, one of which I recall as holding the record for sheer asininity. It drew attention to the fact that the little circles of paper, punched out of folios so that they could be put on files, might be collected and sold as confetti!

But with all this "ragging," G.H.Q. had a very real respect and liking for Brigadier-General Gibbs and his Salvage Corps, and recognised fully the solid and practical patriotism which made them devote a passionate interest to the recovery of solder from old tins, to collecting waste paper, old boots, nails, horseshoes, rags and buttons. "There is nothing of the débris of the battlefield which we cannot put to some use," General Gibbs announced; and by his personal enthusiasm he made Salvage collection quite a popular sport in the Army.

Some of the items of salvage value from a return will show the wide range of the department: swill for piggeries, value 16,000 francs; solder from old tins, value 91,000 francs; cotton waste, 14,000 francs; tin-plate (won by unrolling old biscuit tins, etc.), 61,000 francs; old lead, 10,000 francs; various bye-products 7,000,000 francs. The old rags collected did a great deal to help the cloth shortage at Home, as they made the best kind of shoddy. The old bones collected helped to find the glycerine for explosives.

But perhaps the moral effect of the Salvage department was even more valuable than its excellent material results. War is a wretchedly wasteful business and must inculcate in soldiers a spirit of waste. But in the final phase of this campaign every soldier had brought home to him most urgently the wisdom of saving and the real value of what seemed to be waste bye-products. Many of them must have learned the lesson and carried it home with them to the advantage of the general community.

Agriculture was another economy organisation that we owed to the German submarine war. It had begun in a small way towards the end of 1917; indeed its germ was alive before then, for from the first our units had helped the French with labour and horses during harvest time, and some units enjoying a certain security of tenure had established flower and vegetable gardens. But in December, 1917, the world's food position suggested an earnest effort to utilise spare labour and spare land within army areas in France to grow food. Major-General Ellison and Dr. Keeble came over to G.H.Q. from the War Office, and a scheme was drawn up to cultivate 50,000 acres of

THE ECONOMY SERVICES.

land. In January, 1918, an Agriculture Directorate was formed under Brigadier-General the Earl of Radnor, and search was made for a suitable area for a big farm. The quest was not a simple one. We could not poach on land that the French might want. We wished to avoid selecting an area which might be needed for a manœuvre ground for our troops in the carrying out of the next Big Push. In seeking to avoid these two rocks we landed on a worse one. The area selected around Roye-Nesle was the area which the Germans were going to over-run in their Spring offensive. All unconscious of that, we began ploughing in February, 1918. The Home authorities had supplied an abundance of excellent machinery, and labour was quickly collected and trained. By March 21st we had got up to a record of ploughing 300 acres per day and a total of 4,742 acres had been turned over. Then the German came.

BRIG-GENERAL THE EARL OF RADNOR
(Director of Agricultural Production)

THE ECONOMY SERVICES.

By a fine feat of organisation and courage the Agriculture Directorate saved most of its machinery. Some of the agricultural tractors came in useful as aids to the heavy artillery in the retreat. Others, charging for home at their best speed, were mistaken for German Tanks and in one or two cases fired on by our troops.

Despite that unlucky experience with the big farm, Agriculture put to its credit some useful work. It had promoted vegetable gardens in Base Camps, and the total area of those gardens was 7,496 acres and their products did much to help out the rations. Soon, too, "Agriculture" found that though it had not sown on its big farm it might still reap in other quarters. The German onrush had brought a great area of French cultivated land within army areas, some of it actually within the zone of fire. Since every ear of wheat was precious, Agriculture organised to save this part of the French harvest, and actually reaped the product of 18,133 acres. It was gallant work, done mostly by fighting men in the intervals between their turns in the trenches. Sometimes the area to be reaped was under the fire and the observation of the enemy, and the crop was cut at night. The enemy used gas shells to prevent this work, and the reapers had to work in gas masks. One area of six acres of corn was so close to the enemy trenches that the idea of saving it seemed a desperate one. But volunteers were found, and one night seventeen men with scythes cleared the whole six acres, in the three hours of darkness that were available. I own that such acts of heroism impress me more than deeds done in the heat and ardour of battle.

In the Autumn of 1918 the enemy were in full run for the Rhine, and the Agriculture Directorate resolved to make another attempt at cultivating a big farm. An area of 20,000 acres was chosen, this time near Corbie. The site had been desolated by the Somme battles, and the work of preliminary clearing (which was done by Prisoners of War) was the hardest part of its preparation for agriculture. But when ploughing began with tractors other unexpected difficulties cropped up. The big armour-piercing shell with delay-action fuse, when it missed the emplacement for which it was designed and struck the ground, penetrated to a great depth, exploded there, and often formed a big subterranean cavern without showing any crater on the surface. A heavy tractor going over one of these caverns would break through and disappear. Digging it out would then be a laborious task. When the Armistice came the Corbie farm was, in accordance with the wishes of the French Government, passed over to it. So the

Agriculture Directorate never got in a big crop of its own sowing. But it had done excellent work on its farm gardens and in saving the French crop within the battle area.

Forestry was another department which we owed to the German submarine war. In 1916 shipping losses were already so great as gravely to prejudice the prospects of bringing in timber from Scandinavia. It was Scandinavia which felt the earliest effects from the submarine campaign; Norway, especially, which with fine courage had refused to allow its mercantile shipping to take refuge in harbour.

The Norwegian paper *Tidens Tegn* published an optimistic statistical review of the position as regards Germany's submarine war on October 9th, 1917. This, covering a wide period and dealing with a mercantile service which the German pursued with particular venom, attracted great attention at the time. Pointing out that for the week ending October 9th not one Norwegian vessel was sunk by German submarines, the *Tidens Tegn* commented that this was the first time for a year that such a thing could be said. It gave then in detail the record of U-boats' ravages on Norwegian shipping from May, 1917, until October, 1917, the record showing a steady decrease of losses. But the sad truth was that the Norwegian shipping had suffered such terrible losses that there was not much left of it to destroy.

As early as November, 1916, owing to the difficulties in getting Scandinavian timber, we had decided to draw our timber supplies chiefly from the French forests and from Switzerland, Spain, and Great Britain. Our Forestry Department started with a Canadian lumber-men's unit. Brig.-Gen. Lord Lovat was Director. In October, 1917, a fresh agreement was made with the French Government for the exploitation of French forests for the benefit of the Allied Armies. The magnitude of the operations can be gauged from the fact that the Forestry Directorate grew to 425 officers and 11,000 of other ranks, and employed in addition about 6,000 prisoners of war. But perhaps the public, with Whitehall departments in its mind's eye, may object that employment figures are no sound indication of work accomplished. But the production figures admit of no cavil. From November, 1917, to November, 1918, the Forestry Department produced from French forests 2,065,074 tons of timber. This was four-fifths of the total needs of the Army. Reference will be found in a subsequent chapter to our shortage of barbed wire in the Winter and Spring of 1918. Forestry did a great deal to fill the gap, producing 90,000 tons of defensive pickets between February and May, 1918.

AT FORESTRY H. Q., THE KING AND A MASCOT

In addition to its productive work Forestry was a valuable Directorate in the teaching of economy in forest exploitation. If the lessons it inculcated are not wasted, British forestry should benefit greatly in the future.

Salvage, Agriculture, and Forestry were the three chief "Economy Directorates" of G.H.Q.; and if their spirit can be carried back into civil life by the demobilised soldier it will prove of real value in making up for the economic wastage of the war, vast as that has been. I wonder if those people who are celebrating peace with a long-drawn-out carnival of slackness and extravagance recognise as clearly as we were made to do at G.H.Q. in 1918 the extent to which the world is short of everything! Of course it is difficult for those who are not accustomed to give close attention to the problems of production to appreciate how deeply a world war of four years' duration affects every industry; and especially so when on one side the war was waged on the principle of destroying everything that could be got at, whether it was military or civil property, whether it was an enemy or a neutral possession. Germany, making a ruthless and unlimited war on "sink without trace" lines, forced practically the whole world to band against her in self-defence; and over practically the whole world labour and capital were largely withdrawn from production for purposes of defence.

In the days when the builders of Jerusalem worked with the trowel in one hand and the sword in the other, it may be concluded that progress was slow. For years a great deal of the world had the rifle in one hand and the gas mask in the other, figuratively or literally. It could do little in the way of normal production, because its chief energies were taken up with defence.

In regard to any industry, trace step by step the effect of a war such as this war. The first and most palpable loss is that of the labour directly withdrawn for armies and navies. That would be serious enough if it were the sole loss. But it was only one of many losses. A modern industry depends as much almost on capital as on labour. Capital was withdrawn from production and devoted to destruction at an appalling rate. That meant that industry was starved of machinery, of communications, of nutriment generally. Like a human body deprived of proper nourishment, it began to suffer from debility.

THE ECONOMY SERVICES.

Every neglect to replace machinery, to repair roads or to open up necessary new roads, every draft, too, made on the administrative staff, is just as much a weakening of an industry as the direct loss of hand workers. A healthy industry should be able to withstand for some time these losses, just as a healthy human body should be able to withstand some period of privation and even of actual starvation. But there is a limit to the power of endurance in both cases. It is quite clear that in many world industries (and most particularly in those industries which are connected with the great staples of human comfort, the food industries, the clothing industries, the transport industries) that limit was reached long before the war was over, and the world began to suffer from a constitutional enfeeblement of its powers of production; something more serious than the temporary interruption of production, something which makes now a restoration of prosperity difficult and tedious.

All this is so true as to be truism. But it does not seem to be so clearly recognised by the people who stayed at home as by the people who went to war. Perhaps as the returned soldier makes his influence felt more strongly he will have his value in bringing the nation to a sense of the duty of economy. It was not possible to have two views about the need of economy when you had to forage the battlefield for old bits of metal and rags.

CHAPTER X.

THE COMFORTS OF THE FORCE—SPIRITUAL AND OTHER.

The Padres—The semi-religious organisations—E.F.C. Comforts—Studying the Fighting man—The Great Beer Save.

"There has never been an army that had more chaplains, or that needed them less." That was the verdict of one American observer on the British Army—a sound one. The British Army was notably well supplied with chaplains—"padres" as the soldier knows them; but this was not in answer to a call for spiritual leaders to combat a special degree of wickedness. Quite the contrary. The Army was a very well-behaved, sober-minded institution on the whole, as if it recognised the solemnity of its task and fitted its conduct accordingly. To this fact the French population can bear witness. The French villagers among whom the British soldiers have been quartered came to a view of them which was once eloquently expressed: "They are lions in the trenches and lambs in the villages."

So the padre went out for duty with the troops having no task of leading a forlorn hope against ramping wickedness. His trouble was rather in the other direction. "I don't see how I can have the 'front' to preach to these men," said a padre attached to an Artillery Division one day: "I'd rather they preached to me."

It really was a difficult task—that of the padre at the Front, and only the best type of clergyman made a success of it. His attitude to life had to be manly, his character brave. But the padre who ran risks just for the sake of running them was often more of a bother than a help. The best padre's spirit was that of the careful soldier who will face any danger that comes in the way of duty, but will not go looking for danger in a spirit of bravado. The padre could make two mistakes. He could take things too easily and just be a parson available to conduct Divine service when he was wanted to; or he could try to do too much, to interfere too much and become a nuisance in the fighting line. The good padre struck the happy mean. He had the knack of being there when he was wanted, but he recognised that the Army's first duty was to fight, and he did not get in the way of its fighting activities. Above all he did not try to arrange a church parade for the morning after tired troops from the line had reached rest billets.

One of the most successful padres in France was known as "the Lost Sheep." He had a Mess to which he was properly attached and this Mess was responsible for having a comfortable billet for him. But he was rarely "At home." He wandered all over the district, picking up a meal here and there and sleeping wherever he found himself after dinner. At first it was thought to be fecklessness on his part. As a matter of fact it was artfulness. Moving about as he did, taking a meal and a bed anywhere, he got to know everybody and found out who needed him as padre.

The actual organisation of the padre service was a little difficult for the layman to understand. The "Principal Chaplain" with the Forces was a Presbyterian clergyman, the Rev. J. M. Simms. Under him came all the padres, including Roman Catholic priests, except the padres of the Church of England, who had a separate organisation under a Deputy Chaplain General, Bishop Gwynne, who had been Bishop of Khartoum before the war. What was the exact reason for the division of authority I could never quite make out. There was no ill-feeling at all or jealousy between the various padres. The Principal Chaplain had his headquarters at Montreuil and was a regular visitor to the Officers' Club. The Deputy Chaplain General had his headquarters at Paris Plage.

Of the typical padre it was said that he was responsible for at least as many sports meetings in rest camps as Divine services, but was a genuinely spiritual man withal. There was credited to one the aphorism that the men did so much worshipful work in the trenches that in rest camps the first thing to be rightly thought of was relaxation. G.H.Q. Staff I fear were poor Church-goers. The Commander-in-Chief set a good example by attending Divine Service almost every Sunday at Montreuil, but most of the Staff Officers followed the maxim "*laborare est orare*" and were at their desks on Sunday. The padres understood the position and there were no reproaches.

At meals at the Officers' Club there were always a few padres. We were not expected to make too much concession to "the cloth" in the way of conversation, and the average padre stood his chaffing with the best of them.

I noted one, who had a rather pontifical manner (though he was a thoroughly good fellow at heart), take a hard hit in a sporting fashion.

The conversation had turned on Lord Roberts' campaign before the war to try to arouse the British people to a sense of the imminence of the war and the necessity of preparation. The padre blundered in with:

"It seems to me that Lord Roberts and his friends must have been singularly lacking in clearness of argument and persuasiveness seeing that, knowing the truth as they did yet they were not able to convince the people."

"Yes," retorted an officer, "arguing on the same lines, quite a number of excellent gentlemen seem to have been singularly lacking in clearness of argument and persuasiveness for nearly 2,000 years, seeing that, knowing the greatest truth of all, they have not yet been able to convince the world."

The padre took it in the right spirit and owned that it is not necessarily a reflection on a preacher if his hearers will not listen. Lord Roberts' name was venerated by most officers, and the Army was glad that when the time came for the good old man to lay down his sword it was from among old comrades at G.H.Q. that he passed away.

In addition to the padre service the British soldier in the field had a great number of semi-spiritual organisations looking after him. These followed a sound rule, generally, of providing hot coffee and harmless recreation as the best missionary work. G.H.Q. recognised the Y.M.C.A., the Church Army and the Salvation Army as semi-religious agencies, and all these bodies did excellent work in providing rest huts and reading and recreation rooms for the troops, and thus keeping them out of mischief when they had idle times. Satan, when he came roaming round, found the British Army well dug in, and plenty of wire out.

To some proposed forms of guarding the welfare of the soldier G.H.Q. had to refuse sanction. There were many cranks with very curious notions on this point. Perhaps the most remarkable proposal was that which came from a lady, the goodness of whose intentions was obvious but who had "a marked moral strabismus," as a Scots doctor pawkily observed. She wanted to form an organisation of

THE COMFORTS OF THE FORCE—SPIRITUAL AND OTHER.

ladies (and said she could do so) to meet soldiers at the ports of disembarkation and take them to homes where would be provided all the comforts of domesticity. I believe that some such organisation once actually existed in an Eastern country whilst it was at war. But so far as the B.E.F. was concerned it had to be discouraged.

The last line of entrenchments against ennui and discomfort was provided by that wonderful organisation the Expeditionary Force Canteens. It provided for officers and men cheap shops, good rest and recreation centres, and for officers excellent hotels. The officer thus had never to wander to strange places. From the Expeditionary Force Canteens during the greater part of the time you could buy cigars, cigarettes, chocolate, sweets, all kinds of canned goods and so on, duty free, and at prices far lower than those of the London shops. Whisky and beer could be bought, too, duty free, under some restrictions. The E.F.C. was, in short, the great comfort-bringer to the soldier at the front. I say comfort-bringer, for all necessities were supplied by rations.

Just consider what Tommy got from the country he was serving: an ample supply of meat (fresh meat in the main), and bacon and cheese, of bread, and of biscuit; a fair supply of vegetables, of butter, of jam, of tea, milk and sugar; a moderate supply of tobacco and cigarettes; a small ration of rum. I know from my own experience that one could live excellently on the men's rations. Nothing was actually needed to supplement them. But comforts, well, they were comforting; and the E.F.C. by bringing them almost up to the front trenches (as they did) helped materially to win the war.

The Expeditionary Force Canteens organisation was formed early in 1915 for the supply of canteen facilities to the troops in the field. Its operations commenced in France, but were subsequently extended to all theatres of war. The undertaking was from its commencement conducted by Sir Alexander W. Prince and Colonel F. Benson, both of whom patriotically gave their services. In due course the organisation took on various other functions, but its canteen business alone made it by far the biggest shopping concern in the world. The "supplies and shipping" department of the E.F.C. had for canteens alone an average annual turnover of approximately 500,000,000 francs. From three to four thousand lines appeared on the stock sheets, ranging from a packet of pins to officers' equipment.

The tonnage handled was enormous, and during the month of November, 1918, it reached nearly twelve thousand tons, representing

320,000 cases. But the record week was that ending March 16th, 1918, just prior to the great German offensive, when 3,643 tons of canteen supplies were landed, and a turnover amounting to 10,586,407 francs was reached. The tonnage off-loaded for the year 1918 was 121,000 tons, and comprised over three million packages.

Here is a table of figures of total sales at canteens and depôts:—

Half-year ended	Francs.
June, 1915	3,283,641
December, 1915	18,207,427
June, 1916	48,629,071
December, 1916	104,288,430
June, 1917	150,786,105
December, 1917	191,063,817
June, 1918	223,931,847
December, 1918	223,247,454
Total to end of December, 1918	963,437,792

The E.F.C. was in business for the good of the troops, not to make profits for anyone. All profits that were earned will go back to the soldiers. But profits were kept to a strict minimum. By a happy decision prices for the same goods were the same on every Front. You bought a tin of tobacco at Baghdad for the same price as at Boulogne. Thus the soldier on the more comfortable nearer-home Fronts was able to feel that the little percentage of profit charged to him was helping his mate in Mesopotamia.

Yet another fine feature of the E.F.C. work was that it served the man in the front line first and the man at the Base second. In 1917-1918 the shipping position was so bad that economies had to be effected in every possible direction. E.F.C. supplies had to suffer with the rest, and the complaint came that what supplies did come over were largely absorbed at Base and on Lines of Communication, and the men in the front line got very little. The Q.M.G. got rid of that complaint very simply. An order went out that: (1) certain luxuries which were in very short supply should go only to front area canteens and not at all to the Base; (2) other goods should go in the proportion of four to front areas and one to the Base. As a consequence our

THE COMFORTS OF THE FORCE—SPIRITUAL AND OTHER.

Montreuil canteens were very poorly stocked, for G.H.Q. of course did not count as a front area. But the simple justice of the step was recognised.

In 1918, the Home Government was forced to the conclusion that the shipping position was so bad that no more beer could be consigned to the troops. Beer was a very bulky article and its shipping space must be saved. G.H.Q. did not like the prospect of stopping the soldiers' beer just at a time when they had plenty of other troubles. Perhaps G.H.Q. remembered a much earlier B.E.F. in Flanders in the reign of Henry VIII., which did very badly until that great War Minister, Cardinal Wolsey, took the matter of supplies in hand and saw that the Army was well supplied not only with arrows but with beef and beer. Thereafter that early B.E.F. retrieved its reputation. It occurred to G.H.Q., B.E.F., 1918, that whilst beer is a very bulky article, most of the bulk is water. Accordingly the Q.M.G. took over, in part or in whole, breweries in our Army areas and arranged to brew beer locally, importing only from England the malt and the hops, which were not particularly bulky.

I do not know whether the decision of the Home Government was in part a concession to teetotalism and in part only governed by shipping considerations. If so the teetotallers were disappointed. The British Army in 1918 continued to number beer among its comforts. On the whole ours was the most comforted and comfortable Army in the Field, as all *liaison* officers from allied units agreed. The Americans were as well off in most respects, but being a "dry" Army interfered somewhat with the comfort of its majority. The average American was not a teetotaller and did not object to wine and beer or even an occasional whisky. At his own canteens he had to be. The French of course always had a wine ration, but in other respects their "comforts" were not up to our standard. The privilege that was extended to French *liaison* officers of dealing at our canteens was very highly appreciated.

CHAPTER XI.

THE LABOUR AUXILIARIES.

The queer ways of the Chinks—How to bury a Chinaman properly—The Q.M.A.A.C.s and their fine record—Other types of Labour auxiliaries—The Labour Directorate.

THE Great War revived, to a degree that few dream of, methods of very old campaigns, when the hero had his attendant myrmidons and the Spartan foot soldier his helots. Study a "ration strength" return of the B.E.F., France, 1918, and discover how the actual fighting men in trench or gun-pit had to be supported not only by Base soldiers but by British non-combatant labour companies, by French civilian labour companies, by Q.M.A.A.C.s, by prisoner-of-war labour companies, by Indian, West Indian, Fijian, and Chinese labour companies. It was a big business, this organisation of the labour behind the fighting area.

Chinese labour was of very notable help to the British Army. At its best it was the most efficient and hard-working force imaginable. At its worst it was at least a good source of fun. The Chinaman came over to the war with very definite ideas of making as good a thing out of it as possible. "I sell my labour" was his formula in signing the contract, and, though he probably would not recognise as his own the old British law formula *caveat emptor*, that was the principle on which he acted. If the buyer of his labour was fool enough to pay the price and not get the work that was the buyer's look-out.

Every Chinese coolie on arrival (as we soon found out) was "put wise" by the representative of his secret society, his "Tong," that "this is a good place. You have only to pretend to work." He acted on that, and unless the people in charge knew how to deal with Chinese, so little was done as to make the most finished British exponent of "ca-canny" go green with envy. But, given an officer who knew his business, knew how to get the Chinese headmen to get the Chinese coolies to work, and the results were splendid.

THE LABOUR AUXILIARIES.

The Chinaman knew that by his contract he was not to suffer war risks, that he was not supposed to work under shell-fire, and he was soon sufficiently advanced to interpret an occasional air bombardment as "shell-fire," and to give it as a reason for demanding more pay. As a rule he was willing to take risks, if he were paid extra. When sick or wounded he was a great nuisance, for if a Chinaman died of sickness whilst in charge of the white man the conclusion was that he had been done to death. Ordinarily a sick Chinaman demobilised two workers—himself and some member of his own secret society who had to accompany him to hospital to see that all was fair.

The most earnest effort was therefore made to keep the Chinaman from dying, not only from ordinary motives of humanity, but because as a corpse he was an even greater nuisance. A British soldier might be buried in a blanket, but the Chinese dead had to have wooden coffins, and their graveyards had to be chosen with great care—preferably in a valley with a stream running through it. All this to satisfy the spiritual world of the Chinese, which seems to be very exigent in such matters. The official instructions regarding Chinese graves stated: "The ideal site to secure repose and drive away evil spirits is on sloping ground with a stream below, or gully down which water always or occasionally passes. The grave should not be parallel to the N.S.E. or W. This is specially important to Chinese Mohammedans. It should be about four feet deep, with the head towards the hill and the feet towards the water. A mound of earth about two feet high is piled over the grave."

In matters of finance the Chinaman was also a little bothersome. He had to have his pay right down on the nail; he distrusted any white man's savings-bank or any system of deferred pay. In time Chinese savings-banks were instituted, and these solved the difficulty that the Chinaman would not let the white paymaster keep his money for him, and if he had it in personal custody gambled it away.

Keener even than his passion for gambling was the Chinaman's passion for decoration. Was it in a sense of real fun on his part or was it an accident that his taste for decoration culminated in the two "grand passions"—an Australian hat and a Scotsman's kilt? If either of these came within his reach the Chinaman knew real bliss. One Chinaman who managed to get hold of both at once, and paraded a Base town in their joint glory for a full half-hour was the legendary hero of all the Chinese coolies in France. Of course to be in possession of an unauthorised article of military equipment was an offence, and the Chinaman going out in a kilt or an Australian hat, or a general's red-haloed cap, knew that he was in for severe punishment. That was no deterrent if his ingenuity could secure, by theft or purchase, such glory. As often as it did the Chinaman was quite willing to stand the subsequent racket. One Chinese coolie used to light up a quarter of Boulogne with a decoration that challenged military discipline successfully. He had secured one of those brass basins still used in places as barbers' signs, had fixed this on his ordinary coolie hat, polished it resplendently, and sported it with Celestial pride. His was the brassiest hat of any brass hat in France; but the basin was not an article of military equipment, and authority decided to wink at it. In a hot sun you had to wink with both eyes.

Discipline was good with the Chinese coolies if the controlling officers knew their business and took care to "save face" of the headmen of the gangs. An officer had to see that the headman did not fool him or ill-treat the coolies and then to back up the headman always. If the coolies got to think that the headman was out of favour with the white boss nothing could be done with them. In matters of prohibitions the Chinese language showed a strange inadequacy. It was decided to forbid smoking in labour camps, and a notice "Smoking is Prohibited," was printed in English, German, and Chinese, to be affixed in the compounds. After some months a distinguished visitor, who was (or thought he was) skilled in the Chinese language, pointed out to high authority that the literal translation of the Chinese notice was "Do not get caught smoking." The educated Chinese who had drawn up the notice originally was sent for. He blandly insisted that that was the only way to say "Smoking is Prohibited," in Chinese, and that the Chinese coolie would understand nothing else.

On the whole the Chinaman was a cheerful soul. He organised his own theatrical companies and enjoyed those interminable Chinese operas which are familiar to travellers in the East and to visitors to the Chinese quarters of American or Australian cities.

The "Chink" gambled as much as the regulations allowed him to. But he could stand up to a hard day's work with constant cheerfulness, and, apart from his craze for some prohibited military decoration, contrived to make his uniform picturesque enough. The barber was an important unit of every camp, for Chinese head-dressing is a matter of complicated ritual.

Taking one consideration with another, Chinese labour in France was a success. It released many scores of thousands of men for the

THE LABOUR AUXILIARIES.

fighting line. If the Germans had not thrown in their hand at the time they did, it is probable that another 100,000 coolies would have been recruited in China for France, though most other types of coloured labour were being dispensed with as not being worth while.

Chinese labour has a way of cropping up in British history. It might have lost the Mother Country a whole continent of colonies at one time, when Sir Henry Parkes, a leonine Norfolk peasant who had become Prime Minister for New South Wales, dared Great Britain to veto Australian exclusion of Chinese immigrants. Later it loomed, with vast possibilities of mischief, over South African history. In the Great War Chinese labour appeared again, but this time with no sinister threat of trouble, but very helpful in matters of railway-building and ship-building, and lightening, with a touch of Celestial humour, the grim business of putting the German in his place.

The Labour Directorate had control not only of Chinese Labour but of all other non-combatant working units, except the W.A.A.C.s (or Q.M.A.A.C.s as they came to be called when, as a reply to base gossip about their morals, Queen Mary took nominal command of the corps and they became Queen Mary's Army Auxiliary Corps). Distinctly cruel—though it was probably not meant to be cruel and was only thoughtlessness—was the gossip about the W.A.A.C.s. According to some London scandal-mongers a very large proportion of the Corps qualified for a maternity hospital almost as soon as they got to France. As a matter of fact the standard of conduct among them was very high. They represented at least the average of British womanhood, probably they were ahead of the average, and it would be a libel on our race to discredit them with a charge of looseness.

Nor was it a fact that the W.A.A.C.s were in a position unusually open to temptation; it was quite the contrary. They were busy. The soldiers among whom they worked were busy, and it wasn't a case of the Devil having idle hands at his mercy. Further, the system of supervision was well thought out and excellently administered. The W.A.A.C.s had better guardianship than in the average British home. They lived in settlements, with their own recreation rooms. These settlements were strictly out of bounds for soldiers. All private houses, cafés, restaurants, etc., were "out of bounds" to the W.A.A.C.s. Nor could a W.A.A.C. "walk out" with a soldier in her leisure time except by permission of her officer.

At G.H.Q. there were very few W.A.A.C. clerks or telephone orderlies; but there was a little band of W.A.A.C. waitresses at the

Officers' Club. A better set of girls it would be hard to find, and it is hardly necessary to say that they were always treated with respect and courtesy by the officers. A saying at G.H.Q. was that if you wanted to be sent away suddenly there were two short courses to that undesirable end: one, to curse your general to his face in public, the other to be caught winking at a W.A.A.C. G.H.Q. did not wink at the W.A.A.C.s. We had too much respect for them, too much gratitude for the spirit of sportsmanship and patriotism that led them to come out to France to lead a dull and laborious life for our comfort. It is difficult to imagine what a touch of "England, Home and Beauty" those deft young women gave after experience of soldier orderlies as waiters.

From personal knowledge I can only speak of the W.A.A.C.s at G.H.Q. But I had the best of means of judging their general standard of conduct throughout France. In case of a lapse from grace a W.A.A.C. was retired from the Corps, her uniform was withdrawn and she had a grant of £5 to enable her to buy a civilian costume. There were not many cases of that £5 being paid.

But the W.A.A.C.s, as I have said, did not come under the Labour Directorate but under their own Administrator. Every one else whose job was to work rather than to fight did, and that made "Labour" an extraordinarily interesting department. It had under its control:

> (a) The Labour Corps, including:
> > (i) Labour Companies.
> > (ii) Divisional Employment Companies.
> > (iii) Area Employment Companies.
> (b) Canadian Labour Battalions.
> (c) Middlesex (Alien) Labour Companies.
> (d) South African Native Labour Corps.
> (e) Cape coloured Battalion.
> (f) Egyptian Labour Corps.
> (g) Chinese Labour Corps.
> (h) Fijian Labour Detachment.
> (i) Indian Labour Corps.
> (j) Non-Combatant Corps.
> (k) Prisoner of War Companies.
> (l) French and Belgian Civilian Labour.

The core of the organisation was British loyal labour, men who were too old or too decrepit to fight but who "did their bit" behind the lines, making roads or working at various Army jobs. These were excellent stout fellows, and as they did not object to taking the risk of death for their country, they could be, and were, employed in areas of danger. Another type of British Labour, not so admirable, were the Conscientious Objectors. A few groups of these were employed in France as burial parties, etc. Yet another type was known as the Middlesex Contingent—why that county should have been associated with them I know not. They were men British-born but of German parentage, whose loyalty was suspect. They could not be trusted in the army; they were used for some types of labour, but were not allowed near ammunition dumps or other points where they might do mischief.

Second in order of merit came French and Belgian civilian labour, men too old or decrepit for the fighting line, but willing to work for a wage. It was a condition of their employment that they should not be stationed within range of long-distance shell fire, but this condition was sometimes relaxed at their own wish and with the consent of the French Government. At first the British Army insured these French workers against accident, illness, and death through the French State Insurance Department. Subsequently it was found more economical to insure them directly.

German prisoners of war labour was under the Labour Directorate, and in the organisation of it some very good work was done. Prisoners were very plentiful from 1916 onwards, and the Labour Directorate, when a new push was mooted, made its plans to have skeleton prisoners-of-war companies ready to be filled by the new prisoners as they arrived. I think the record was in one case when three days after some Germans arrived at our "cages," they were at work on the roads at the rear of the Army. It was the law that prisoners of war should not be employed anywhere near the firing line, and on the British side this law was very strictly observed.

My impression of the Germans as road labourers was not very favourable. They seemed to loaf as much as they could. But some of the German prisoners of the artisan class did excellent work in our various shops and factories at Base. In tailoring shops, motor repair shops, etc., there were many German prisoners who seemed to take a delight in intelligent industry. German prisoners were very well treated and got on very well with their guards.

Now to the various classes of coloured labour. The Chinese I have already dealt with. They were quite the most satisfactory on the whole.

The Indian labour was willing enough but did not stand the climate so well. Kaffir labour proved on the whole unsatisfactory, and so did Egyptian labour. A West Indian contingent did fairly good work. A model lot were the Fijians, all volunteers (and all Christians, by the way), and wonderfully good stevedores. Unfortunately there were very few of them and they did not stand the climate well. One of the Fijian Labour Corps left his studies at Oxford University to join up.

The Labour organisation had two main objects:

(a) To release the fighting soldier for his legitimate work.
(b) To assist the Services and Departments to carry out their tasks.

Nine hours was the normal working day, exclusive of the time occupied for meals and for going to and from the place of work. If the distance from the place of parade to the work was more than 1½ miles, the time taken to march the excess distance was deducted from the hours of work. For labour of low medical category the normal working day was eight hours.

Excellent work was done by the Labour Corps. Its *morale* was carefully studied and it was part of the instructions to officers that:
All ranks should have briefly explained to them the object of the work, for what, and by whom, it will be used, what purpose it will serve, and, especially, that all the work is being done for the prosecution of the war and is not merely a "fatigue." A few minutes spent in rousing the men's interest in their work is usually time well spent. A healthy spirit of emulation should be created by pointing out the quantity of work of any kind which should be done per day, and the amount done by other and better Companies. Above all the men must be made to understand that whether they are working on time, or on task work, no slacking can be allowed. The men in the fighting line depend on the men of the Labour Corps to keep them supplied with all they require.

Our Allies are just as anxious for victory as we are. The French and the Belgians have suffered more than we have, but, in spite of it, never complain. Hence they should receive every consideration at our hands. As we are in their countries we should respect their customs and wishes as much as we can. In all our relations with any of our Allies, it is obviously desirable for us to be polite and courteous in our dealings with them. It must be borne in mind that every misunderstanding or unpleasantness tends to weaken our alliance and to help the enemy.

THE LABOUR AUXILIARIES.

The Labour Directorate, with many different races to manage, their religions and food habits to study, had one of the difficult tasks of the war; and carried it out on the whole very well. The chiefs of the directorate in my time at G.H.Q. were Colonel (now General) E. G. Wace, Lieut.-Col. S. G. L. Bradley, and Lieut.-Col. H. A. H. Newington, with Colonel Fairfax as Adviser, Chinese Labour, and Colonel Pritchard as Adviser, South African Labour. The staff was about equally divided between big business men and typical Oxford men. It was always a pleasure at dinner to sit at the same table with the "Labour" people. They hunted, or rather dined, in couples as a rule, a leading light of the commercial world pairing off with one of the "Oxford group." So one could always reckon on good talk and argument from opposite points of view.

At the summit of its strength the Labour Corps mustered 387,000, a great Army in itself, and it had representatives of almost every European nationality, Chinese, West Indians, Pacific Islanders, Kaffirs, Zulus, Burmese, Egyptians, Maltese and almost every Indian race including Nagas, Pathans, Chins, Manipuris, Bengalis and Santals. And the Labour Corps' patriotism cost it dear at times; for sometimes it had over a thousand casualties in a month.

Photo by Bassano Ltd.
BRIG-GENERAL E. G. WACE
(Controller of Labour)

CHAPTER XII.

G.H.Q. AND THE "NEW ARMY."

What G.H.Q. thought of the "Temporaries"—Old prejudices and their reason—The material of the "New Armies"—Some "New Army" Officers who did not play the game—The Regular Army Trade Union accepts its "dilutees."

WHAT did G.H.Q., whose view may be taken as the authoritative one, think in 1918 of what used to be known as "the New Army?" G.H.Q. in 1918 represented in the main the pick of the old Regular Army. Nearly all its senior officers were "Regulars." The majority of the junior officers were "Temporaries." What was the feeling between them after the mutual knowledge that the years had brought?

Often I talked this over at dinner, sometimes with men whose opinions I had known in 1914 and 1915. There was H——, for instance, who, in those early years of the war, was an unsparing critic of the "New Army" which was, he used to say then, slovenly and a makeshift sort of show and could not salute properly, and suffered, and always would suffer, from the "non-military mind."

The non-military mind, according to him, was an affliction which was born in one, like original sin, and could only be exorcised by going to a Military Academy and becoming a Regular Soldier. I used to be very meek and long-suffering with him (he was senior to me) and only occasionally mentioned people like Blake (a civilian whom Cromwell made a General, and afterwards an Admiral, and a right good General and a right better Admiral he was) or non-militarily-minded men like Botha and Smuts.

But to what argument I did venture upon he was impervious. I noted that fact for him and quoted it as, perhaps, a characteristic of the mind which was *not* non-military. And altogether we had some charming quarrels, as amusing, almost, as those of old men in their clubs, who if they could not bicker could not digest their dinners, and then where would they be?

G. H. Q. (MONTREUIL-SUR-MER)

Now H—takes it all back. He is at last convinced that the New Army is all right. Of course it is. Why should it not be? Is not the British Empire all right? And is not the New Army a sort of Representative Assembly of the British Empire?

G.H.Q. in 1918 saw clearly enough that never before in the history of any Empire was such splendid raw material for an Army gathered together as in Great Britain in 1914-1918. There were things to offend dainty tastes in the recruiting campaign of which the New Armies were the harvest. But nothing can spoil the value of the result, that many hundreds of thousands of the best men who ever served in an Army joined the colours.

Judge the New Army by the standard of the "Regulars."

The soldiers of the first Expeditionary Force (the "Regulars," the men who, despite the booming of certain special units, did the greater part of the heroic work of Lord French's command up to Loos) have proved themselves so nobly that it is possible to say now, without fear of offence, that if they had been judged as individuals before they joined the Army, they might not have been held to represent the best average of the British people. There is nothing ungracious in saying this now, when even the furious and blinded foe is compelled to admit their excellent virtue. The men of the old Regular Army themselves would admit almost unanimously that it was the Army that made them, and that they occasionally took the King's shilling for lack of prospect of another shilling. The people of England must confess, on their part, that they rather boasted of "not being a military nation" and were content with an army system which did not seek to levy fairly upon the average manhood of the nation but trusted chiefly to the patriotism and instinct for rule of an officer class.

The material of the ranks was not bad material, nor even poor material. The British blood is a good brew. For it has tapped the most adventurous and hardiest veins of the Celt, the Anglo-Saxon, the Scandinavian, and the Norman; and this British blood learned by some subtle alchemy to draw always fresh savour and wholesomeness from the girdling sea. Put out of consideration a few criminal degenerates, and the mentally emasculated politicians who used to preach the gospel of no nationalism, and no British stock is actually bad stock, as can be seen from the superb young nations that have sprung, partly from its lees, in the Dominions.

But the raw material of the New Armies represented a great improvement on the raw material from which was built up the old army. Other things being equal, therefore, the New Armies could be expected to beat the Expeditionary Force. Other things, unfortunately, were not equal, such as officers' education and time of training. But in all the circumstances the New Armies, after some blooding, might be expected to attain, and actually did attain, the high standard set in the field by the British Regular.

The material of the New Armies was such as no recruiting sergeant in 1913 could have hoped to secure. In a fairly typical batch of recruits which I had to take over one day were engine-fitters, brass finishers, coal miners, agricultural labourers, gamekeepers, two foremen, one compositor, one valet, one pugilist (a champion), one stud groom, one cycle mechanic, one clerk. The wages of these men before they joined was high, and only two out of thirty-eight had been of the "usually unemployed" class. Among these men, accustomed to the discipline of the workshop, many of them with experience as gangers or foremen, possible non-commissioned officers were sprinkled thickly. I have seen batches of recruits for the old army just when they joined, and they looked usually rather forlorn—men accustomed to be unemployed, men at a loose end, disappointed men, with just a sprinkling of eager men taking to the soldier's life for the love of it. Only after three months of the wholesome life, the wholesome food, the kindly discipline of the Army, would they fairly compare in physique, manhood, and intelligence with the recruits of the New Armies.

A well-marked stream coming to join the flood of New Army recruits was that of British men from overseas. The British blood is strangely responsive to the magic of the seas. Send a careless young Englishman abroad to Australia, South Africa, or to some foreign land such as China or the Argentine, and the salt air of the seas as he traverses them seems to set tingling in his blood a new keenness of Imperial pride. His outlook comes closer to that of the Elizabethan Englishman. Perhaps it is from the first actual consciousness of what it means to be one of a nation which is mistress of the seas. Perhaps one must seek deeper for a more transcendental explanation, finding it in something analogous to the Greek myth of the giant who renewed his strength whenever he touched Mother Earth.

Let the reason be what it may, the fact is clear enough. Of British men abroad—I speak now of British born, not of those born citizens of the Dominions—one can dare the guess that ninety-nine out of a hundred turned their thoughts at once to the joy of service on the outbreak of this war.

G. H. Q. (MONTREUIL-SUR-MER)

In a city of China I know there were 18 young Englishmen in various commercial houses. Of them 17 came away home to the war. In most cases it meant abandoning their positions and all their future prospects. Money was scarce, and the little band travelled steerage. To realise how great a sacrifice that was, one must know the tropics and the disgusts of having coolies for fellow-travellers. From the Argentine, from Canada and the United States, from New Zealand and Australia, the English streamed home to serve. From such a place as the Argentine there was almost a stampede of British men of fighting age.

Starting with a big handicap of quality in their favour, the men of the New Armies very soon found that it was all necessary if, within the much briefer time allowed them to become fit for the fighting line, they were to succeed in keeping level with the soldiers who would be their comrades. The recruits of the old Regular Army before the war came into an organisation which was officered, from brigade generals down to junior subalterns, by specialists. Officers were drawn mostly from a class with a tradition of rule, and were given a very close training. Those who came in as officers from circles which had not that tradition were in a minority, and during their course of training learned to conform to the pattern set. Very much of the success of the British Army has been due to the qualities of courage, coolness, and *noblesse oblige* of the officers. As a class they gave the best of leads—a far better lead than did the generally domineering, sometimes brutal, German officers. The recruits to the New Armies did not have the advantage of coming to an organisation fully officered by men with this tradition of command and technical knowledge of their work. They had to rely for officers on material which was slightly poorer on the average.

The officers of the New Armies came from five sources:—

1. A few officers spared from units at the Front and devoting themselves to the dull but glorious duty of helping on the new men. These were usually first class.

2. "Dug-outs." A "dug-out" is not a form of entrenchment or shelter but an officer who, having completed, as he thought, his soldier's work, volunteered back to service in the New Army. Some of the dug-outs were up to the standard of the Regular Army and, having kept abreast of modern military progress, were able to "take post" from the outset. Other dug-outs were more or less behind-

hand with modern military science. A few were frankly deplorable. But the "dug-out" in the majority of cases made an excellent officer after a little schooling (sometimes without). Lots of him were at G.H.Q. Sometimes he proved valuable only for the preliminary work of regimental organisation, and was then remorselessly passed over when his unit was finally put into shape for the Front. He bombarded the War Office with furious protests, then took up the licking into shape of another raw unit.

3. Promoted non-commissioned officers from the Regular Force, nearly always proficient in their technical work, and in the majority of cases with also a sound instinct of leadership.

4. Recruited officers from the Universities and the public schools. Almost invariably they had a sense of leadership. They had learned a tradition of rule. In most cases they soon learned the technical part of their work.

5. Recruited officers from the bulk of the community: in many cases very good; sometimes just passing muster; in a few cases distinctly poor. The necessity of a weeding-out was soon recognised. Summing up in regard to the officers of the New Armies it has to be admitted that they came below the standard of the Expeditionary Force, but not much below the standard: and that they got to the standard of the Territorials.

Put to the test of getting a post at G.H.Q., which was supposed to be the crowning test of efficiency, the New Army Officers did not do badly. I made a rough poll one night at the club dinner. More than half the officers present were "New Army" men. In what may be called "specialist" branches New Army men predominated.

The very wide sweep of the net which gathered in recruits gave the New Armies a very varied stock of knowledgeable men to draw upon. The ideal army officer should be, besides a gentleman and a skilled tactician, a good horse-master, a good house-keeper, and a clever mechanician, able to train men, to repair a telephone, a saddle, a cooking-pot or a wagon. No one man can have all that knowledge in perfection, but with the New Armies it was possible to get within a unit men trained in civil life to every form of skill wanted. A regiment, with average luck, would have recruits from the most varied industries and trades, and the picked specialists in time got to "staff jobs" as a rule.

G. H. Q. (MONTREUIL-SUR-MER)

The "Regular" in 1914 and early 1915 was, I suppose, pretty generally convinced that there was not much hope in the "Temporary." Especially was this conviction firm in the mind of the very junior Regular. The "Shop" boy, the young second lieutenant just from Woolwich, had a blighting scorn for the "Temporary," whom he called a "Kitchener" and often affected to regard as not an officer at all but some sort of stranger whom you had to admit to Mess and tolerate in uniform because authority said so, but who obviously was not a "pukka" military man, for he could not talk about his "year" or exchange stories about wonderful "rags." The average senior Regular probably thought very much the same sort of thing, but, having cut his wisdom teeth, did not allow it to show so palpably.

There was a certain amount of justification for this feeling, for the advent of the huge number of "New" officers made a vast change in the social conditions of the Army. It soon became obviously necessary that the Temporary "Pip-Squeak" should come under a severely motherly eye—that of the War Office and of various private philanthropic agencies who would have us all dull and good (and if we cannot be both we can be the one at least). That eye then also glared upon the Temporary lieutenant and other Temporary officers of more exalted grade, and also, to their intense disgust, on permanent officers, who professed to understand why the "Temporary" should be the victim of sumptuary regulation, but not the "pukka commission" man. All these officers agreed that it was the wickedness of the Temporary Second Lieutenant (otherwise Mr. Pip-Squeak) that had caused all the trouble, and could not understand why authority did not recognise this view and make their new rules apply only to the most junior officers. But the rain of rules fell on the just and the unjust alike, and some of the just were wroth.

I could sympathise a good deal, even if I laughed a good deal more, at the officer who found himself "treated like a child," as he put it. The dignity of the position of a British officer in the old Regular Army *qua* officer was remarkable. His officer's rank gave him the confidence of his banker, of his tradesmen, of society generally. To see a British officer in uniform with doubtful company or under doubtful circumstances was almost unknown. The tradition of the officer clan was jealously guarded by the system of training. When at last, having got his commission, Mr. Regular Pip-Squeak reported to his regiment in the old days he found himself still very much in leading strings. Until he had won six months' standing his safest attitude, even in Mess, was that of "don't speak unless you are spoken to." Justice he could expect from his brother officers, and sympathy too, but the sympathy was tempered by severe snubbings to restrain any tendencies to effervescence. Above all things, he was trained to respect his uniform; and as he had generally the right to wear mufti when off duty, this high respect was more easy than in war time, when uniform had to be almost constantly worn.

With the first recruiting of the New Armies, commissions were freely issued to men with no training, and in some few cases with no manners. For a little while a bewildered public did not appreciate the change, and bankers, tradesmen, hosts, had some unhappy experiences. But what may be called the "commercial" aspect of the question was soon put right. Officers' rank ceased to give credit rights. Socially, the readjustment was far less easy. The War Office was at last compelled to assist that process of readjustment with various restrictive orders.

"We have been asking for it," commented one officer grimly when some particularly repressive regulations were published. And without a doubt we had been asking for it—that is to say the conduct of some officers had made not merely advisable but necessary a degree of motherly (or grandmotherly) supervision. Exhortation preceded regulation by many months.

Afterwards commissions were only granted after some service or a Cadet term of training. But the stringent regulations, which offended the dignity of some "Regulars," remained. It was not that a milk-sop standard was aimed at. It was not the case that leave was only given to go out to Mothers' Meetings, Sewing Circles, and High Teas in Presbyteries. It was recognised that boys will be boys. But there is a time when parents must be parents; and the War Office was in this case *in loco parentis.*

But all that in 1918 was an old tale and mostly a forgotten tale. At G.H.Q. there was no scorn at all left for the Temporary who had done his share of fighting, even when he joined the scarlet-tabbed ranks of the elect. He was accepted as a brother officer with the fullest cordiality.

"Very much more interesting show, the Army is now," confessed one Regular Colonel to me. "Talk in Mess now *is* talk. You've no idea how solemn and stuffy a Regular Mess could be, say in India or in a garrison town."

There remained a little good-humoured chaff still for the Temporary who had jumped to a high appointment without any real soldier life at all. Brigadier-General ——, the eminent expert in ——, who became a General very suddenly, was reported to go around partly in dreadful, partly in proud anticipation of a guard turning out for him when he wandered from G.H.Q. area.

The chaff was good-humoured. It was never put under the nose of its object. So it did not do much harm. In truth I was struck by the general good temper with which the Trade Union of Officers ultimately took its "dilutees."

But without a doubt the Officers' Trade Union, or rather the Amalgamated Society of Officers, Non-Commissioned Officers, and Men of the Regular Army, was rather inclined to give the cold shoulder to the "dilutees" in Lord Kitchener's time. These New Army people had not put in their proper term of apprenticeship, had not paid their Union fees. Should they be treated as full members of the Society? But that feeling died away as the blood-bond of a stubborn campaign broadened and stiffened. It could not even be kept alive by the somewhat silly advertisement in some quarters of Territorial units and New Army units and Colonial units at the expense of their Regular brethren.

THE BOULOGNE GATE
From the town

CHAPTER XIII.

G.H.Q. AND THE DOMINION ARMIES.

Our Parliament at the Club—A discussion of the Dominions, particularly of Australia—Is the Englishman shy or stand-offish?—How the "Anzacs" came to be—The Empire after the War.

IT was quite a little Parliament in its way, the Officers' Club at Montreuil, and one of its pet subjects of discussion was the Dominion soldier and the effect that the campaign would have on British Imperial relations. The talk covered a wide field and was sprinkled with anecdotes; it came up many evenings out of all sorts of incidents.

"The Dominion men, many of them, are too touchy," says an officer who has come back from a *liaison* visit. "A Canadian officer—the talk arising out of I do not know what incident—complained to me to-day: 'The Canadians do not seem to take on with the English.' 'Well, the Canadians have a very taking way with them at the Front,' I replied, hoping the allusion to Vimy Ridge would soothe him. But it didn't. I hear from the Australians, too, the same complaint—that the English people 'do not like them.'"

"What greedy young men they are," comments another. "What more do they want than the abject Anzac-worship and Canadian-worship among the British people? If anything ever went to the heart of the old Mother Country and dimmed her spectacles for her, it was the way in which the colonial troops came into the fighting line."

A Dominion officer at the table hazards that the British do seem "stand-offish" until you know them.

A British officer explains that the English are a shy people and a people with a high ideal of personal liberty and individualism; that the Englishman loves a corner seat in a train not so much because it is more comfortable but because it leaves his shyness, and his desire to keep himself to himself, safe on one side; that he does not like to be bothered, that he is very shy from the fear of bothering other people.

G.H.Q. AND THE DOMINION ARMIES.

"Those cold English passing you awkwardly by, my huffy Australians or Canadians, are very proud of you, and they do not go up to shake you by the hand and say so because they fear you would take it as a liberty."

A staff officer who did *liaison* work between Australians and the British during the first battle of the Somme thinks that one of theresults of the Somme was the moulding during its course of a truly Imperial Army. Forces of differing types went into the cauldron. One type came out. All did a full share in the offensive, and by what they taught and by what they learned had their influence in moulding this "Imperial" Force. He blamed some newspapers for having devoted well meant but mischievous energy to spoiling the work of this amalgamation. A good deal of newspaper effort, if it had been taken seriously, he says, would have fostered among the various troops a spirit of third-class theatrical jealousy, as if they were a mob of people competing for public favour and public notice: "Since the issue has been raised in other quarters, let it be said that between Dominion troops and British troops there was a fine emulation in skill and courage, and that no sound judge could give the palm to any one section over another. There were differences in method of courage and skill, no differences in degree."

We all agreed on that; and that the spirit of comradeship between all was firm. Someone noted as a curious thing that there seemed to be an understanding that what is known among soldiers as "chipping" should be dropped in inter-imperial relations. A Durham might explain—with no real but all apparent seriousness—how lucky it was for the Yorks to have the Durhams to lean upon; and the Yorks would respond in kind. In the next trenches a New-South-Waler might, with a vigour that concealed well the want of earnestness in his *blague*, explain the hopelessness of the Victorians. But between British, Canadian and Australian this "chipping" was dropped. They were good comrades, but felt that their mutual intimacy had not yet grown to a stage which allowed of "ragging" or "chipping."

Officers' Club G.H.Q. was inexhaustibly interested in the "Anzacs." They were frequently under discussion. There was far more talk of them than of their fellow colonials, the Canadians. They seemed to have more dramatic interest. Their rakish hats challenged notice, and their rakish actions.

Almost every day there was some fresh yarn of the Anzacs, a yarn of some fine feat told admiringly, a yarn of some classic bit of impudence told tolerantly. One tells a tale of the Anzacs' curious ideas of discipline. Another caps this with the reminder that the Australian corps has the best Salvage Record in the Army—that is to say is the most industrious in rag-picking, shell-case gathering, waste-paper collecting, and so on.

"I don't wonder," the first speaker retorts. "They're always after records. They'd go over and raid the Boche trenches for Salvage sooner than play second fiddle."

"They did marvels saving the French harvest this year under shell-fire."

"Yes, they are all right if you keep them busy. But they are the very devil in rest camp. Now in Cairo——"

But the table refuses to hear the story of Cairo again, because it is not a very pleasant story.

The conclusion I came to is that the British officer had really a very soft spot in his heart for the "wild Colonial boys"—Canadians and Australians. I was always being appealed to, as knowing Australia, to "explain" the Anzac, which I did at great length on various occasions, and here is the substance of it all:

The Anzac striding—or limping—along with rakish hat and challenging glance, for the first time brought Australasia actually home to the Mother Country. These Australasians, the men of the Bush, were as remarkable, as significant almost, as the Dacians in the army of another Imperial nation two thousand years ago. Easily can they be picked out. They walk the streets with a slightly obvious swagger. When they are awed a little, it is a point of honour not to show it. When they are critical a little, it peeps out. Two by two, they keep one another in countenance and are fairly comfortable. Catch one alone and you may see in his eyes a hunger for a mate, a need for some other Anzac. For all his *bravura* air, the Anzac has no great self-confidence; and he has a child's shy fear of making himself ridiculous by a false step. The same fear makes him difficult to know. He will often set up, as a protective barrier against a real knowledge of him, a stubborn taciturnity, or a garrulous flow of what Australasians call "skite" and Londoners call "swank."

In pre-war days an Australian in England might have felt himself a little of the barbarian in so smooth a comity, where people loved moderately and hated very moderately; walked always by paths; were somewhat ashamed of their own merits and suavely tolerant of others' demerits; and were nervous of allowing patriotism to become infected with the sin of pride. But England at war understood them better—the Anzacs, the young of the British. The young of the British, not of the English only, though that is the master element of the breed. The Anzac is a close mixture of English, Scottish, Irish and Welsh colonists, with practically no foreign taint.

There is, however, a wild strain in the mixture. One of the first great tasks of Australasia was to take the merino sheep of Spain and make a new sheep of it—a task brilliantly carried out. A concurrent task was to take black sheep from the British Isles and make good white stock out of them. The success in this was just as complete. The "rebels" of the Mother Country—Scottish crofters, Irish agrarians, English Chartists and poachers—mostly needed only full elbow room to become useful men. Even for the Micawbers a land of lots of room was regenerative.

Was it Charles Lamb's quip that the early population of the British Colonies should be good "because it was sent out by the best judges?" That was a truth spoken in jest. The first wild strain was of notable value to a new nation in the making. It came to Australasia not only from the original settlers but also from the rushes to the goldfields. And—note here the first sign that the Anzac people were to be dominated by the British spirit and were to keep the law even while they forgot conventions—there was never a Judge Lynch in an Australasian mining camp. The King's writ and Trial by Jury stood always.

The Anzac started thus with good blood. To carry a study of the type to the next stage, to note how the breed was influenced by environment, it is necessary at the outset to put away the idea that the Australasian people are engaged, to the exclusion of all other interests, in the task of subduing the wildnesses of their continent. They have done, continue to do, their pioneer work well, but have always kept some time for the arts and humanities. To ignore that fact is, I think, a common mistake, even in the days when every European opera-house of note had heard an Australasian singer or musician, every European salon had shown Australian pictures, and there was even a tiny representation of Australian Art in pre-war Montreuil.

"Does anybody in Australia then have time to read Greek?" a schoolmaster's wife in England asked once with surprise.

G. H. Q. (MONTREUIL-SUR-MER)

She was answered with another question: "Who is the great Greek scholar of the day?"

"Professor Gilbert Murray."

"Well, he is an Australian."

It was a specious argument, for one swallow does not make a summer. But the truth—that Australasia produces at a high rate mental as well as physical energy—could have been proved categorically.

The Australian is not only a pioneer wrestling with the wilderness. He is a creature of restless mental energy, keenly (perhaps with something of a spirit of vanity) eager to keep in the current of world-thought, following closely not only his own politics but also British and international politics; a good patron of the arts; a fertile producer and exporter of poetasters, minor philosophers, scientists, writers, and artists. There is nothing that the Anzac, nationally, resents more than to be regarded as a mere grower of wool and wheat, a hewer of wood and digger of minerals. He aspires to share in all the things of life, to have ranches and cathedrals, books and sheep. Above all, perhaps, he has a passion for *la haute politique*.

All this was in the blood. The "wild strain" was not only of men who found in the old country a physical environment too narrow. It was partly of men who desired a wider mental horizon. Some very strange minor elements would show out in a detailed analysis of early Australasian immigration—disciples of Fourier who gave up great possessions in England to seek an idealistic Communism in the Antipodes: recluse bookworms who thought they could coil closer to their volumes in primitive solitudes. But one element was strong—the political and economic doctrinaire; and the conditions of the new country encouraged the growth of this element particularly, so that Australia soon won quite a fame for political inventions (*e.g.*, the "Australian Ballot" and the "Torrens Land Title"). But the general growth of what may be termed a "thinking" class was encouraged by the very isolation which, it would seem at first thought, should have an opposite effect. Whilst other young countries lost to older and greater centres of population their young ambitious men, Australasia's antipodean position preserved her from the full extent of the drain of that mental law of gravity which makes the big populations attract the men who aspire to work with their brains more than with their hands. Australasia will always be claiming attention not only as a producer of wheat, wool and well-knit men, but also of ideas.

The ideas of this young nation of the British, nurtured in the

G.H.Q. AND THE DOMINION ARMIES.

Australasian environment, would strike the pre-war England of five years ago as naively reactionary. The Anzac, faced by natural elements which are inexorably stern to folly, to weakness, to indecision, but which are generously responsive to capable and dominating energy, had become more resourceful, more resolute, more cruel, more impatient than his British cousin. The men who followed the drum of Drake were much akin to the Australasian of to-day.

Australian Imperialism, in truth, must have had for some years past a fussy air to the cooler and calmer minds of England; though the good sense and good humour of the Mother Country rarely allowed this to be seen. When New South Wales insisted on lending a hand in the little Soudan War she was not snubbed. Nor was Victoria, pressing at the same time a still more unnecessary naval contingent. In the South African War Australian eagerness to take a part was more than generously recognised, and when Australia next insisted on giving help also in the suppression of the Boxer Rising, room was patiently found for her naval contingent.

About this here is an illustrative story, which is welcomed as "quite Australian." When the Australian Gunboat "Protector" arrived in Chinese waters the British admiral went on board to pay his compliments and was not stinting in praise of Australian military and naval prowess. Thereupon the Australian band is said to have struck up with a tune from "The Belle of New York:" "Of course *you* can never be quite like us."

It is perhaps a true story; certainly possible. There is a touch of gay impudence in the Australian character which an ex-Governor confessed he loved "because it was so young."

Always one comes back to that word "young." It is the key to an understanding of the Anzac—youth with its enthusiasms, rashnesses, faults, shynesses; youth, raw, if you will, but of good breed and high intentions.

Australasian life leads to a certain hardness of outlook. Life is prized, of course, but its loss—either of one's own or of the other fellow's—is not regarded with any superstitious horror. Certainly it is not regarded as the greatest evil. To go out with a mate and to come back without him and under the slightest suspicion of not having taken the full share of risk and hardship would be counted greater. Living close up to Nature (who can be very savage with tortures of fire and thirst and flood), the back-country Anzac—who sets the national type—must learn to be wary and enduring and sternly true to the duties of mateship. The Bedouin of tradition suggests the Anzac in his ideals of mateship and of stoicism. The Anzac follows the same desert school of chivalry in his love for his horse and dog and his hospitality to the stranger within his gates. He will share his last water with the animal he is fond of; and in the back-country the lonely huts of the boundary riders are left open to any chance caller, with a notice, perhaps, as to where to find the food stores, and to "put the treacle back where the ants cannot get to it." It is, of course, a point of honour not to take except in case of need.

An English padre who put in two years in the "Back of Beyond" of Australia as a "Bush Brother" confesses that his first impression was that the Anzac of the Bush was cruel and pagan. His last impression was that the Anzac was generally as fine a Christian as any heaven for human beings would want. An incident of this parson's "conversion" (he related) was the entry into a far-back town of a band of five men carrying another on a stretcher. The six were opal miners with a little claim far out in the desert. One had been very badly mauled in an explosion. The others stopped their profitable work at once and set themselves to carry him in to the nearest township with a hospital The distance was forty-five miles. On the road some of the party almost perished of thirst, but the wounded man had his drink always, and always the bandages on his crushed leg were kept moist in the fierce heat of the sun. One of the men was asked how they had managed to make this sacrifice.

"It was better to use the water that way than to hear the poor blighter moan."

Many a night we speculated to what degree the different Dominion types will approximate as a result of this war. Certainly when the Dominion and British troops were in contact tidal currents of knowledge flowed to and fro which left both the gainers. Points which had been particular property became common: regarding economy in the use of the water-bottle, the art of making a bed in a shell-hole, informal methods of acquiring horses, the best tracks towards the soft side of Ordnance, the true dignity of salutes, sniping as a sport, the unpatriotism of recklessness, and other matters. Slang was pooled and trench language much enriched. In all things the essential kinship of the British race was disclosed.

We agree that after the war, the British Empire will have more of a general likeness. Colonial ideas will have penetrated more strongly into the Mother Country. British ideas will have permeated the Colonial restlessness and impatience. What an ideal race the British could be with a constant coming and going from the Mother's home to the children's houses; an exchange of good grey wisdom with eager enthusiasm, the equable spirit of green and cloudy England mingling with the ardency of the Dominions.

Finally a Dominion officer sums up:—

"I do not think an Empire managed on the old British lines could survive another great shock. It is charming to be so equable and good-tempered and to love your enemy as yourself and to do good to those who hate you. But it brings a nation too close to the fate which overcame the Peruvians under the Incas (they were a charmingly equable and good-tempered and confiding race). Yet those who hope for an Empire managed on Canadian lines, or on Australian lines, leave me cold. I want good wheat crops and cathedrals, the best of the new and of the old spirit. And just as the sole real advantages of being rich are that one can be honest and generous, there would be no use at all in being a great Empire and yet not feeling strong enough to 'play the game' fairly and chivalrously. I hate hearing the talk—which is the swing back from the excess of British tolerance—of a cold-blooded and merciless efficiency as the ideal of national life. Better to perish than to be a German Empire trampling on the faces of women and babes to the throne of power."

CHAPTER XIV.

EDUCATING THE ARMY.

The beginning of an interesting movement—The work of a few enthusiasts—The unexpected peace—Humours of lectures to the Army—Books for the Army—The Army Printery.

IN the last phase of the war G.H.Q. saw a remarkable new development in Army organisation: the inclusion of civic education as part of the soldier's Army course. Before this war, of course, there had been Army schoolmasters, and these in peace time did valuable work in teaching illiterate soldiers. Cobbett, we know, owed his education to the Army; so did one of the famous Generals of this war, Sir William Robertson; and once we had as a visitor and lecturer at G.H.Q. an American University Professor whose first education had been won as a ranker in the British Army.

But the new Education Scheme had a much wider scope than the old Army schools. The plan in brief was to make civic education a definite and compulsory part of Army life, so that every man joining the Army should have a course of humane and technical or professional education. The plan is now in course of being carried on to successful fruition, and in the future the Army will be a Continuation School as well as a defence service.

This may prove to be one of the most useful results of the war. It was due to the enthusiasm of a little band of soldiers and civilians, the leaders of which were Colonel Borden Turner, Major-General Bonham-Carter, Colonel Lord Gorell and Sir Henry Hadow.

The Army Educational movement had a small beginning with the organisation of lectures. After the fighting of 1917 it was felt that something more than the usual round of cinema shows and the performances of Divisional theatrical troupes was necessary to help to recreate the fighting value of the Army, and that what was required was something more solid and intellectual, something that would raise an interest in civic subjects quite apart from the war. It was therefore decided to get as many scholars as possible to come out and give lectures to the men. During the previous winter the Y.M.C.A. had arranged for a few lecturers to come out and lecture in back areas, and they had machinery already existing for looking after them in France. The Y.M.C.A. now again undertook the work of housing, feeding, and transporting the lecturers in France, and for all arrangements for getting them to the country. Major-General Bonham-Carter persuaded some of the Government offices, viz., Reconstruction, Food Control, Pensions, Labour, Education, to send out men who could help the movement; and Lieutenant-Colonel (then Captain) Borden Turner came to G.H.Q. to supervise the details. All arrangements for lectures were made by the General Staff with the Y.M.C.A. Lecturers were sent to units in the fighting areas rather than to the Lines of Communication.

MAJOR-GENERAL C. BONHAM CARTER

EDUCATING THE ARMY.

Later on it was decided that we must have an organisation to carry out a big scheme of general education directly an armistice was declared, so that the time of the men might be profitably employed while waiting for demobilisation after the fighting was over. This decision was made in December, 1917. Major-General Bonham-Carter and Captain Borden Turner worked out a scheme with this idea, and Sir Henry Hadow, an educationalist of great renown, gave his assistance. Already efforts in this direction had been made in England and in the Canadian Corps and elsewhere by individuals, to provide facilities for education and hold classes, and a few voluntary classes were being held by the Y.M.C.A. There was, however, no organised effort anywhere except in the Canadian Corps.

In January, 1918, it was decided to get the scheme started as early as possible and not wait for the Armistice. But at that time there was a great shortage of men, and naturally any scheme which demanded new establishments met with objections. For this reason things moved slowly. However, a scheme was got ready, waiting for the favourable moment to arrive. It arrived sooner than was expected. At an historic dinner one night at Lord Haig's château his personal enthusiasm was aroused, and he gave orders for the preparation of a scheme for general education throughout the Army in France with the object (1) of making men better citizens of the Empire, by widening their outlook and knowledge, (2) of helping them by preparing them for their return to civil life.

Lord Haig approved of the scheme that had already been prepared, but it was put into force slowly, because very few men could be spared from fighting and Lines of Communication work to fill the establishments required. But a start was made. The scheme arranged for the work to be administered by General Staff officers and attached officers in all Formations, but on the Lines of Communication the Y.M.C.A. carried out all teaching work as agents of the General Staff. In April, 1918, it was realised that the efforts in France would be greatly hampered if they were not co-ordinated with those in England and elsewhere. The War Office was therefore urged to undertake this co-ordinating work. Lord Gorell, who was at that time working under Major-General Bonham-Carter in the Training Branch at G.H.Q., was appointed to the War Office for the purpose.

The Army Education movement had warm sympathy from those at the head of affairs. The Commander-in-Chief when once it was put before him was enthusiastic. So was Lord Milner, then Secretary of State for War; and Sir Travers Clarke, Q.M.G. and Major-General Daunay (Staff Duties) gave it every support. But it was a movement from below rather than from above, a movement springing from a widely-spread feeling amongst the soldiers that they should win some better outlook on life from their term in the Army.

If one man more than another should be singled out in this movement, which really sprang from spontaneous generation, it would be Borden Turner. He had the crusading spirit and preached Education to every authority until what was a vague aspiration came to be a concrete fact. Certainly Borden Turner was a scarcely tolerable friend to many of the already over-busy officers at G.H.Q. He was always urging them to give lectures, to take on classes. At this time there was practically no "Establishment," and the only hope was to get officers to give spare time to educational work. They had no spare time, but at the remorseless urging of Borden Turner they stole hours from sleep or from the Ramparts and gave lectures or took classes.

Before the Armistice the Organisation of the Education Branch had progressed to some extent. Lord Gorell had gone to London and found a sympathetic leader in Major-General Lyndon Bell, the Director of Staff Duties, War Office, and S.D. 8 was established, having as its chief officers under Lord Gorell, Sir Henry Hadow, Colonel Sir Theo. Morrison, Major Basil Williams (the writer of a famous Life of Chatham), and Major Frank Fox. General Bonham-Carter and Lieutenant-Colonel Borden Turner remained in France, and the work of the new branch was being established and co-ordinated with that of the Y.M.C.A. and with the Canadian, Australian, and New Zealand Army Education schemes when the German unexpectedly threw in his hand. A feverish rush for demobilisation at once set in. As a consequence of newspaper agitation the original demobilisation plans were seriously upset, and one of the worst sufferers was the Army Education movement. Still an amount of useful work both on the humane and the technical side was effected. Best of all, the principle was firmly established that if a nation takes away a young citizen from civil life it owes it to him that when the time comes to send him back to civil life it will not be into a blind alley; his term in the army will be employed to make a sound citizen of him and to give him training in some vocation.

The Army Education organisation set itself to search out teaching talent in the Army before calling in outside assistance, and it made some interesting finds. Many a University don was discovered in a

LIEUT-COLONEL D. BORDEN TURNER

very humble position. A gentleman described as "one of the most learned men in Europe" was a bombardier in a battery. N.C.O.s and rankers who were Fellows of famous colleges were common enough. Most of them were drawn into the Education organisation.

One of the officers taken by Education from G.H.Q., where he was a staff captain in the Adjutant General's Branch, was Captain Hansell, who had been the Prince of Wales' tutor in his student days. Hansell, in addition to his scholarship, is a sagacious urbane diplomat with a deep and sympathetic knowledge of French life. He would have been best placed on the Military Mission to the French Army. But that would have been a serious loss if it had taken him away from G.H.Q., where his after-dinner talk cheered the seniors and his artful unobtrusive tutelage helped the juniors. Captain Hansell took charge of the Lecturers' Headquarters for Education, and the task must have made a very heavy demand on his tact. Lecturers of all kinds were being sent out to France to address the troops, some of them with very vague notions of what was required of them in the way of kit. One lecturer vastly pleased his soldier audiences, but imposed a heavy strain on transport by always appearing on the platform in full evening dress. Another lecturer went out—in a Flanders winter— with a frock-coat as his warmest garment, "and it was the thinnest frock-coat in Christendom," observed a sympathiser. Of course a very great deal of "roughing it" was the lot of the lecturer going from unit to unit to troops living under active service conditions.

Moreover organisation was not perfect at the time. At one period a steady stream of lecturers was arriving at Lecturers' Headquarters but none was going out to lecture, because all transport for the time was absorbed in a particularly heavy phase of demobilisation.

The lecturers, on whose damask periods idleness was as a cankering worm in the bud, got into a sad state of impatience and were threatening to lecture one another, or do something else desperate, when the position was saved by a timely visit to them of the Prince of Wales and his brother, Prince Albert, who had tea with them, chatted over their work, and convinced them that they were not out on a fool's errand. Shortly afterwards the transport situation was relieved, and the lecturers rushed to their audiences and peace reigned again. But it is dreadful to think of what might have happened if there had not been the urbane and diplomatic Captain Hansell smoothing over troubles. A mutiny of lecturers would have afforded some puzzling problems to the Provost-Marshal.

CAPTAIN H. P. HANSELL

G. H. Q. (MONTREUIL-SUR-MER)

Before the Army Education organisation was born a great number of men in the Army did some good solid reading. The Camps Libraries organisation in England sent out to every unit parcels of books.

Most of these were of the opiate class, light magazines and light stories intended to bemuse and not to educate the mind. But a proportion of good books slipped in and were warmly appreciated by some.

The Army itself had a very fecund printing press, but it was devoted almost solely to the production of books of orders and regulations and text books. Regimental annuals of a humorous kind existed but were not encouraged. As a rule they were printed in England, not in France, and the conditions of censorship—more perhaps than the taste of writers and readers—confined them as a rule to somewhat feeble japes.

There were very often mooted proposals for a G.H.Q. Monthly. It might have drawn on a very distinguished band of writers. But authority contrived that these proposals should never come to maturity. The expenditure of time and material was grudged, and G.H.Q. was naturally very nervous on points of "Intelligence." There are a thousand and one ways in which military secrets can be given away with quite harmless intent. An Intelligence General's aphorism on this point ran: "We find out far more from the stupidity of our enemies than from the cleverness of our spies."

It is clear that silence is the one sound policy. If a man says nothing, nothing can be discovered from him. If he will speak, even it is only with the intention of deceiving, he may disclose something. British diplomacy abroad (which was not such a foolish show as some critics say, or else how comes it that the British Empire, from the tiny foundation of these islands, has come to its present greatness?) was always the despair of the inquisitive Foreign Correspondent, for it never said anything. An Embassy or Ministry which would tell a lie, especially an elaborate lie, was far preferable, for from something you may deduce something; from nothing, nothing. G.H.Q. acted with a sound discretion in smothering all proposals for a G.H.Q. Monthly.

The Army did most of its own printing, of maps, orders, forms, and training books. Maps were done by the R.E. mapping section, other printing by the Army Printing and Stationery Services under Colonel Partridge. This was a highly efficient department with printing presses of the most modern type at Boulogne, Abbéville, and elsewhere. A.P. and S.S. printed daily General Routine Orders and, as occasion demanded, poured out in millions Army Forms, posters, pamphlets, and books. Both the French and Americans used its services. It could print in Chinese and Arabic as well as in European characters, and some of its achievements in the way of quick and good printing would do credit to a big London printing house.

The Boulogne Printing Press, which was under the care of Major Bourne, was a particularly up-to-date establishment much praised by the Americans and the French as well as by our own Army. It put a strain once, however, on the politeness of the French. The French Mission at G.H.Q. wanted a book printed giving a record of its organisation. A.P. and S.S., in the right spirit, did its best to make the book a handsome one, and designed a special cover with *fleur-de-lys* decorations. The French Mission, with tact but with firmness, pointed out that France was now a Republic and a monarchical symbol could hardly be permitted on an official publication. It might give rise to a suspicion that the Army contemplated a *coup d'état*. The printers regretted and tried again. The second cover design bore the good old Roman Republican device of the lictors' fasces. But they were shown reversed. The French were desolated at being so exiguous, but could something else be tried, just plain type? The printers were determined, however, to give the good French something to show what an artistic people we English really are, and made a third effort at a decorated cover. This showed a really charming design in which the Gallic Cock strutted triumphantly along a rose-point border. The French were enchanted, so enchanted that they found reason to have another book, an annexe to the original book, printed with the same cover.

American Army publications were normally somewhat more solemn and staid than our own. Occasionally, however, the American humour broke out, as in the gas warning leaflet, which had not, perhaps, the sanction of American G.H.Q. but was widely (and usefully) circulated in the trenches. It began:—

> In a Gas Attack
> There are only Two Crowds
> The Quick and the Dead
> Be Quick and get that Gas Mask on!

After the Armistice, the Printing Services, no longer so much pressed with other Army work, were able to undertake some purely educational printing. But by this time demobilisation was sweeping away the classes, and the best of the opportunity had passed.

CHAPTER XV.

THE WINTER OF OUR DISCONTENT.

The disappointments of 1916 and 1917—The collapse of
Russia—The Cambrai Battle—The German propaganda—
Fears of irresolution at Home—Reassurances from
Home—Effects of the Submarine war—An economical
reorganisation at G.H.Q.—A new Quartermaster General—
Good effects of cheerfulness at Home.

THE Somme campaign, 1916, had been begun with very high
hopes. The main conception of it was a sound one, to attack the
German line at the point of junction between the French and
British forces, the point where, according to all the accepted principles,
the Allied line should have been weakest but actually was not. That
was the only way to bring an element of the unexpected into a grand
attack in those days of long and laborious artillery preparations. (The
Tank did not appear on the scene until the Battle of the Somme was
two months old and did not develop its usefulness as a substitute for
artillery preparation until nearly a year later).

For the Somme battle an enormous artillery concentration was
made, and a special "Army of Pursuit" was trained in the rear of our
lines to follow through when the German line had been breached.
Then there was a preliminary bombardment of the German positions
from the sea to beyond the Somme, and, amidst many feint attacks,
the British and the French offensive north and south of the Somme
was launched.

The First Battle of the Somme made the walls of Jericho quake
but just failed to bring them down. The Army of Pursuit was given
no chance of pushing to the Rhine; its energies had to be diverted
towards sustaining the attack. The fighting season closed in 1916 with
the Germans still holding their main defences but convinced, so far as
the reasonable section of their leaders were concerned, that the game
was up and that the best thing to do was to work for a peace on the
best terms possible.

ON THE RAMPARTS

G. H. Q. (MONTREUIL-SUR-MER)

Thus 1916 was a somewhat disappointing year; 1917 was even more so. The fighting season, that year, closed with the Allied cause in a worse position than in 1916 and with Germany correspondingly encouraged. There would have been some reasonable excuse if in the winter of 1917-18 tails drooped at G.H.Q. The weather was particularly vile. Every day the winds that howled over the bleak hill-top seemed to have come straight from Russia and Germany, bringing with them a moral as well as a physical cold. The casualty lists of the Autumn were not cheerful to ponder over; and it was singularly depressing to hear from Home that in some political circles those casualty lists were being conned over with the idea of founding on them a case against the Army.

Nobody was inclined to try to represent the late Autumn campaign as altogether satisfactory. But it was felt by the soldiers that "they had done their durn'dest, angels can do no more;" and that there was not sufficient appreciation of the fact at Home that with Russia down and out, France in a very bad way, Italy tottering, the British Army had had to step into the breach, had had to take a gruelling without being able to accomplish much more than defence.

It had seemed in 1916 that the time had arrived for Germany to pay the penalty. But a triumph not of a military kind came to her rescue. The German methods of espionage and civil corruption were on the whole as blundering and as disastrous as her other methods during the Great War. They helped to alienate practically all the civilised neutral world. But in Russia—mystic, generous, trusting Russia—they had an unhappy success. In the Autumn of 1916 this first showed. Roumania at that time joined in the war against Germany, and this new accession of strength apparently marked the near end of the war. But Russia mysteriously collapsed owing to the effects of German corruption. Roumania was left "in the air," and a large part of her territory was over-run. From this date, though many of the gallant soldiers of Russia made heroic efforts to safeguard their country's honour, that great Ally was practically out of the fight. By the winter of 1917-18 she was quite out. The French had had grave troubles. The Italians had had to send out an S.O.S. signal.

We should have been more cheerful if the Cambrai attack, 1917, had had the full success it deserved. That really was in its conception and execution a very fine affair. At the time Germany was drawing troops and guns from the Russian Front and pouring them on to our Front in wholesale fashion. Both France and Great Britain had had to send Armies to the help of Italy. Our Battle of Passchendaele was not exactly flourishing. To undertake a new battle was the last development the enemy expected of us; and to do what is absolutely unexpected is to do the big thing in war. The British command collected an Army ostensibly for Italy, made a great secret assemblage of Tanks, and suddenly attacked the Germans in the strongest part of their Hindenburg line. Their line was particularly strong at that point. It comprised three series of defences each one covered by triple barriers of wire from 50 to 60 yards deep. A system of dug-outs (constructed with the labour of Russian prisoners) at a depth of 50 feet below the surface made an underground city with water and electric light installations, kitchens, drying-rooms and the like. Above the surface the houses were closely packed with the earth removed from the excavations, and thus became great earthworks indestructible by any shell-fire.

All this the British Third Army, in a surprise attack carried out by the Tanks and the Infantry, over-ran and captured in a day's attack. So fierce was the British advance and so feeble the German defence *when taken by surprise* that we almost got into Cambrai. If that centre had been won the German Front in the West would have been deprived of its central pillar. The German defence, however, rallied in time to avoid absolute disaster. When the German military mind was given time to think it could always make a good show, and the *riposte* to our Cambrai attack was a good one. We lost most of the fruits of a dramatic *coup*. It was more than annoying to think that just when we had successfully solved the problem of a break-through we had not the means, owing to commitments elsewhere, to push the thrust home.

Cambrai was a good deal "boomed" in the English Press at the time on "popular" lines. But I do not think that the skill of generalship and organisation that it showed were quite appreciated. The favourite British pose of being a complete ass, altogether inferior to the "other fellow," used to be pushed to the extreme point in regard to military matters. The British had a quaint humility in respect to their military skill. In a shame-faced kind of way they admitted that their soldiers were brave; but for examples of military genius they always referred to the "other fellow." Yet one may be daring enough, perhaps, to say something on the other side; and to suggest that in the Great War the German was really surpassed in most points of military skill by the

G. H. Q. (MONTREUIL-SUR-MER)

British. The difference was not always great, but where the difference was greatest was just in those points of invention, of new tactics and new strategy, which show the better brain. Heresy it will seem; but the truth is that from 1914 to 1918 the British military system showed itself superior to the German in resource and sagacity. Perhaps it would be better to say the British-French military system, for it is difficult to separate the achievement of one from the other.

Consider one by one the main features of the great campaign. The warfare in the air was its most dramatic feature. Everything of air tactics and strategy that the German used he copied from the British and French. It was the British who originated aeroplane attack with incendiary bullets on captive balloons, aeroplane escort of attacking infantry, aeroplane sallies at low altitude on enemy trenches, and the various combinations of observing machines with fighting machines. In the first battle of the Somme, when the British and French first disclosed their sky tactics, the German was absolutely driven out of the air. He had then to learn to copy all our methods; and he originated none of his own.

Another dramatic feature, the complicated and terribly effective artillery curtain fire, was evolved by the British-French command. It was copied by the Germans, who themselves contributed nothing new to artillery science during the war. Yet another leading feature was the Tank, the Tank which made its real value first felt at Cambrai. This was a purely British invention, evolved during this war for the needs of this war.

Our "Winter of discontent" was not made any sweeter by the suspicion that existed of a possible yielding on the part of the political powers at Home to German propaganda. This German propaganda took the form of blazoning the preparations for a sensational Spring offensive in 1918; it was trumpeted like a Fat Woman at a Fair, and supplemented by an almost equally strident advertisement of a gigantic defensive. In addition to preparing a great on-rush in which Calais, Paris, Rome, and perhaps London were to be captured, the German High Command wished the world to know that it was also preparing a mighty series of defensive positions back to the Rhine. Wonderful showmen! They had not only the most marvellous Fat Woman, but also a miraculous Skeleton Man. And the prize they wished to win,

166

by bluff if not by fighting, was agreement to an inconclusive peace.
The soldiers were not affected much by these tactics. They took solid
comfort from two facts. The first fact was expressed in the homely
proverb "Much cry, little wool." Had the Germans been confident
that they could smash through the steel wall which barred them on
the West from the sea, from the capitals of civilisation, and from the
supplies of raw material for which they were starving, there would
have been no preliminary advertisement. The effort would have been
made, and Germany's enemies would have had to abide by the result.
There would not have been any compunction at the consequent cost
in blood. The mere extravagance of the advertisement of the German
plans was proof to the soldiers at G.H.Q. that those plans were
recognised not to have a solid enough military foundation, and had
to be reinforced by showy bluff.

The second fact which gave solid comfort was that in any
comparison at all of forces the German group was inferior to the
West European-American group. There was not any doubt at G.H.Q.
Indeed the more the Germans protested of what they were going to
do in the Spring of 1918 the more firm was G.H.Q. in believing that
the enemy was at last coming to the end of his resources and was
anxious to "bluff" a peace rather than "show" a weak hand.

But it was feared that the people at Home might take the other
view, and it had to be admitted that the German put up a very strong
bluff. Perhaps its cleverest form at the time was in the discussion
of "peace terms"—a discussion in which it was presumed that the
German would impose a victorious peace before the summer of 1918.
A characteristic discussion—G.H.Q. kept a close eye on the German
press and minutely examined every German paper published during
the war—would begin with some Prince pointing out the minimum
indemnity that Germany should exact from her foes, and explaining
in what form it should be exacted. Germany's need, it would be
pointed out, would be for raw materials, food, cotton, wool, rubber,
tobacco, silk and the like. It was these that must be supplied to
Germany by way of indemnity. They would have to be supplied not
free, but at a price 20 per cent. lower than the current market price,
and the annual value of this discount would only reach the modest
sum of £50,000,000 a year.

To have had to provide yearly a tribute of any kind to Germany
would of course have taken away the independence of the Allies
completely. They would have been put in the position of admitting

a German suzerainty, and would have become as the oppressed Christian provinces of the old Turkish Empire. But to provide this tribute of raw material, the discount on which at 20 per cent. would be £50,000,000 a year, would have been to engage to send to Germany yearly raw materials of her choice to the value of £250,000,000. This would have been the first call on the farms, the mines, the shipping of the Allies, and only after that call was met would the Allies have been able to begin to supply their own larders and their own factories.

That was one direction the German Peace Propaganda took. The idea of it was, presumably, to strike terror into our hearts, to make us welcome with something like relief the actual official terms of a peace negotiation when they came to be promulgated.

Then someone in Germany would take the other side. Assuming with absolute cock-sureness that Germany must win the war in the Spring of 1918, this publicist would affect to regret the savage terms of peace imposed upon Russia. These terms, it was argued, did not represent the con sidered wishes of the German people. But in war the wisdom of the statesmen was pushed aside by the eagerness of the soldiers. The German politicians were overwhelmed in regard to the Russian peace because the Russian had allowed things to go too far. But if only the Western Powers would agree to negotiate for peace *now,* the "reasonable German politicians" would be able to assert their authority. There would be no ruthless military conditions such as were imposed upon Russia. Sweetly and moderately the Germans would frame their terms; but the Powers of the Entente must "put the war into liquidation at once." Delay would mean that the "reasonable German politicians" would lose their power to restrain the military party.

G.H.Q. remembered the old fable about certain trustful animals being invited to pay friendly visits to the cave of a beast of prey. One wise animal noticed that whilst there were many tracks of visitors going into the cave there were no tracks of visitors coming out. We had noticed that a free Russia went into negotiation with Germany to conclude a friendly and reasonable peace on terms of "no annexations and no indemnities." No free Russia came out.

But G.H.Q. was honestly alarmed for a time that resolution would be shaken at Home, and welcomed with joy (as the Germans did with rage), the firm declarations of the Versailles Council of the Allies and the unshaken confidence and resolution shown in the speech from the Throne at the prorogation of the British Parliament.

THE WINTER OF OUR DISCONTENT.

As soon as the Home political situation was seen to be clear, G.H.Q. set about preparing for the "wrath to come" with a good deal of cheerfulness and with some amusement that the German propaganda should, as a final kick, make a strong though forlorn effort to revive the old story that Great Britain contemplated the seizure from France of Calais and the department of Pas-de-Calais. "Even," said the German Wireless about this time, "if it is not openly admitted that the English will never voluntarily evacuate the French port of Calais, which they have occupied—" etc., etc.

This lie revived in our Mess between British and French *liaison* officers an old topic of humorous conversation. For when this particular lie was burdening the German Wireless some time before, a British General was showing to a French General the arrangements of the British Base at Etaples. He exhibited with pride the great bath houses for the men, built of concrete and "good for a hundred years." "Ah yes, very solid—good for a hundred years," said the French General, laughing. Then they both laughed.

Christmas, 1917, was celebrated with the usual British merriment at G.H.Q., and on New Year's Day everybody's cheerful greeting was "That this year may see the end of the war." But I think there were few officers of standing who thought that a peace Christmas was possible in 1918. No one would contemplate the possibility of losing the war, of stopping on any terms short of a German surrender; but few could see any possibility of victory near ahead. There were thick clouds all round the horizon. Russia was finished. Italy was not cheerful. France was recovering but not yet showing sure signs of emergence from that fit of depression out of which M. Clemenceau was to pull her—the soul of a Richelieu in his frail body.

The worst symptom of all from the point of view of the British Army was the threat of a shortness of supplies. Just when the collapse of Russia had allowed the enemy to concentrate his full strength on the Western Front, the great reservoir of British wealth, which was the main financial resource of the Alliance, showed signs of not being inexhaustible. There was a call at the same time for greater preparation and greater economy. From the beginning of 1918 there were two great cross-currents of correspondence between G.H.Q. and the Home Government, one demanding new weapons, new defences, new equipment, the other demanding rigid economy in steel, in timber, in shipping space, in food, in oil, in expenditure generally. This was partly due to actual lack of money and of credit. But in the main it was the result of the submarine war.

It was at the end of 1915 that the German Admiralty prepared a memorandum arguing that if unrestricted submarine war were adopted as a policy (*i.e.*, sinking everything, hostile or neutral, warship or passenger ship), then Great Britain would be compelled to sue for peace within six months. The memorandum gave various statistics regarding food supplies, tonnage, etc., to prove this hypothesis. The memorandum was forwarded to the Imperial Chancellor, and by him sent to Dr. Helfferich, Secretary of State for Finance, for a report. Dr. Helfferich reported adversely. He was not convinced that Great Britain would be brought to her knees. He feared the effect upon neutral nations of such a policy.

The German Admiralty persisted in its view. Thereupon the matter was submitted for report to ten experts representing finance, commerce, mining, and agriculture. These experts were asked to advise (1) as to the probable effect upon Great Britain (2) as to the probable effect upon Germany's relations with neutrals and (3) as to how far the situation in Germany demanded the employment of such a weapon.

All these experts agreed that the effect on Great Britain would be to force her to sue for peace within six months or less. Indeed, Herr Müller, President of the Dresden Bank, thought that Great Britain would collapse within three months. All the experts also agreed as to the third point of reference, arguing that Germany's position was so difficult that the most desperate measures were necessary to end the war. Herr Engelhardt, of Mannheim, Councillor of Commerce, thought the economic position of Germany so bad that a few weeks' delay might render even ruthless submarine war useless. On the second point, the effect on relations with neutrals, the experts were divided. Some thought that the United States would be driven to war, others thought not. In all cases they did not see a reason against ruthless submarine war in their possible relations with any neutral.

But the fateful decision was not taken until February, 1917, when the destruction of peaceful shipping, whether of enemy or of neutral countries, was ordered. It did not end the war in six months, nor in twelve months; but by the beginning of 1918 there were some very serious difficulties of supply just when the strictly military position demanded the most generous effort.

I wonder if those experts who bandy to and fro explanations and accusations in regard to the German break-through in the Spring of 1918 ever have looked at the matter from the point of view of supply, of the supply, say, of one sternly necessary item of defence, wire? At a careful computation we wanted 12,000 tons of barbed wire in January, 1918, and 10,000 more tons in February, 1918, to give our men a reasonable chance of holding the line which we knew to be threatened. Of that total of 22,000 tons we actually got 7,700 tons, *i.e.*, 35 per cent. of what was needed.

I do not quote this fact to start another quarrel, shuttle-cocking blame from soldier to politician. I am more than ready to believe that the people at Home were then doing their best (as, *pace* all grousers, I believe they did their best from August, 1914, to November, 1918). But you cannot spin out wire like you spin out talk, especially barbed wire. The British soldier can, with his mere flesh and blood, and that gay courage of his, do wonders in the way of making up for want of material. But he could not hold up the attacked sector in the Spring of 1918 against overwhelming odds; and one of the reasons was that he had not enough wire in front of him. He had not the wire in front of him because it had not been, *could not be*, supplied.

How anxious was the task of G.H.Q. at the dawn of 1918 may be illustrated with these heads of correspondence, in and out.

> To G.H.Q. from Home.
> The greatest economy in steel is urged.
> The position in regard to shipping is serious; the strictest
> economy in everything is necessary.
> Lubricants are hard to get. We urge the greatest economy.
> From G.H.Q. to Home.
> More machine-guns are urgently needed.
> There is a shortage of blankets; there is a shortage of
> 8,000 tons of barbed wire. New searchlights are needed;
> 300,000 box respirators are needed for the American Forces.

I could fill many pages with matter of the same sort. The poison of the submarine war began to have its cumulative effect just when we were getting the most peremptory reminders that Supply was going to be the determining factor of the final struggle, that war had become more and more a matter of striking at the enemy's life by striking at "the means whereby he lives." Munitions, food, equipment, railways, roads, ships—these had become the most important factors, and victory would incline to the Force which could best concentrate the means to maintain an overwhelming force at some particular point, which could best develop, conserve, and transport its material. The field for the strategist had moved more and more from the Front line towards the Base.

Fortunately, the British Army in France had for its Q.M.G. at this crisis a man with the courage and the knowledge to carry through a drastic reorganisation of the Supply and Transport services. Lieutenant-General Sir Travers Clarke, who took over as Q.M.G., France, at the end of 1917, was a daring experiment on Lord Haig's part; for he was a comparative youngster to be put into a post which was then the most anxious and onerous in the Army, and his actual substantive rank was that of a major; but he was an acting Major-General with a fine record in a minor theatre of the war. Lord Haig knew his man well, though, and, what was just as necessary, knew how to back his man. He put Sir Travers Clarke in the saddle and kept him there in spite, I have no doubt, of many thunderous protests from influential quarters, for Sir Travers Clarke was a ruthless reformer and a stubborn upholder of any course of action he thought necessary. A character sketch of him that appeared in the *Morning Post* in 1919 is worth quoting in part:

LIEUT-GENERAL SIR TRAVERS CLARKE

G. H. Q. (MONTREUIL-SUR-MER)

"'That big young man,' was a leading American officer's term to describe Sir Travers Clarke after he had met him in France in Conference, and had not caught his name. British G.H.Q. perhaps only learned to appreciate the Q.M.G. fully from the comments of foreign officers who came into touch with him in 1918. The masterful man took his power so quietly, came to big decisions with such an air of ease, such an absence of anything dramatic or violent, that it was a little difficult to understand his full strength.

"'T.C.'—as often before remarked, the British Army must reduce everything and everyone to initials—as a regimental officer in the 'Nineties never seemed to get an opening. Nor did his early Staff work bring him much recognition. But an officer of his to-day, who was a clerk under him when he was first a Staff Captain, insists that he always gave the impression of great power in reserve. 'He believed in the British Army, in hard work, and in himself.' That was the foundation of the career of a man who, once an opening showed, forged ahead with marvellous speed to his destiny.

"It took 'T.C.' ten years to become a major; within the next ten years he had become Lieutenant-General and Quartermaster-General to the British Armies in France. One year in that post, a year in which were crowded all the experiences that a great Army could have, marked him as a great leader of men and a superb organiser. How much the Allied victory owes to him a grateful country will not appreciate fully until not only the British but also the French and American campaigns are analysed.

"'T.C.' had the ideal personality for a military leader. You were always dreadfully afraid of him and sincerely fond of him. No general ever made sterner demands on his officers and men. If you could not stand up to a gruelling day's work and come up smiling for the next day's and the next day's, until the need had passed, you were no use, and you moved on to some less exacting sphere. But you were working under a worker, and you found yourself part of a massive machine which was rolling flat all obstacles. That made it easy. Further, there was the most generous appreciation of good work and a keen personal sympathy.

"Sir Travers Clarke has one rule to which he never permitted an exception: that it is the fighting man who has to be considered first and last. In France he was quite willing that the Staff should labour to the extreme point of endurance to take any of the load off the man in the trenches. He did not like about him men, however clever, who had

174

not seen fighting. It was the first duty of the Staff, he insisted, to enter with the completest sympathy into the feelings and the difficulties of the fighting man. 'Bad Staff work mostly arises from not knowing the differences between an office and a trench,' was one of his aphorisms."

This is not a history of the war; nor a contribution to any of the numerous war controversies; it is merely a sketch of life at G.H.Q. as it appeared to a Staff Officer; but I cannot help obtruding a reply to some current criticisms of Lord Haig: that he was too inclined to stand by his officers, that he was reluctant to "butcher" a man, and that in consequence he did not get the highest standard of efficiency. Faithfulness to his friends and servants was certainly a marked characteristic of Lord Haig as Commander-in-Chief. He chose his men cautiously and, I believe, with brilliant insight. Having chosen them he stood by them faithfully in spite of press or political or service thunderings, unless he was convinced that they were not equal to their work.

It is a characteristic which, even allowing that there was an odd case of over-indulgence, of giving a man a little too much benefit of the doubt, worked on the whole for the good. Men do not do their best work with ropes round their necks; and I believe that a great newspaper magnate whose motto at first was "Sack, Sack, Sack," very soon found out that it was a mistake.

In this particular instance I suppose the Commander-in-Chief had powerful urging often enough to "butcher" his Q.M.G., who did things of so disturbing a character. He did not; and the event proved him right, as it did in practically every one of his great trusts during the war.

Reorganisation of Supply and Transport filled the attention of G.H.Q. during the early months of 1918. Over a curiously wide range of subjects swept a wave of reform and retrenchment. As I have already told, there was a definite organisation to collect the salvage of the battlefields, an organisation which saved millions of money in rags, bottles, waste-paper, swill, bones and grease as well as in the more obvious matters of shell-cases and derelict arms and ammunition.

G. H. Q. (MONTREUIL-SUR-MER)

An Agricultural Directorate was set to work to grow potatoes and oats and vegetables and other food stuffs behind the lines. Rations were judiciously reduced, a substantial difference being left in favour of the man in the actual fighting line as compared with the man at the Base. The supply of certain luxuries at the E.F. canteens was stopped or limited, but it was provided that the man in the fighting line should suffer less from this than the man at the Base. Weekly conferences were instituted to discuss the most economical use of labour, of material and of plant. Every matter great and small had searching attention, and the British Army began to be run like an up-to-date competitive business. Some of the injudicious laughed. They christened the General in charge of Salvage "O.C. Swills" and "Rags and Bones." They could not "see" a Colonel whose mission in life was to cut down laundry costs and arrange for the darning of the men's socks when they came out of the wash.

But all these things had to do with the winning of the war. It is a fact that if the lavishness of 1914-15-16-17 had been carried into 1918 we could not have won the war, because we should have been bankrupt of material.

G.H.Q. at the dawn of the Spring of 1918 was very serious in mind, but not so much so as to fail to get some amusement as well as interest out of the various new ideas in military administration; and fully confident now that the people at Home were going to stick it out. In this connection there was often mentioned with cheerfulness a London bye-election towards the end of 1917 for an area which had had special attention from the German air-raids. Some rather expected to see a candidate come forward from among the little group known as "Pacifists," who would seek votes on the plea that the best way to stop air-raids quickly and to get out of the discomforts of the war would be to meet half-way the proposals of the Germans who were trying for an inconclusive peace.

What actually happened was quite different. A candidate came forward under the banner of the Government, pledged to the Government's programme of carrying on the war until German militarism was crushed and Germany made reparation for the ruin she had wrought in Europe. This candidate had the support of both the old political parties. Against him there came out another candidate. Did this candidate seek to win votes by pleading for a friendly consideration of Germany's hypocritical peace proposals? He did not. From what one could gather of the feeling of the electorate, if he had done so he would have been ducked in the nearest pond. No, his appeal was based on the plea that the Government candidate did not go far enough in hostility to Germany, and that that gentleman was not fully in favour of carrying to German homes the dastardly air-war which Germany waged on a civilian population.

Then a third candidate appeared on the scene. He was not for any half-hearted policy. His cry to the electors was that neither of the other two candidates was sufficiently earnest in regard to the war against Germany. His programme was of one clause only, the necessity of bombing Germany out of her barbarism. He did not believe that any method of sweet reasonableness was of any use. A thousand tons of bombs daily on Berlin, and a ration in proportionate scale on other German towns, was his idea.

Women speakers came to take part in the contest. Did they advocate making concessions to the German desire to sneak away from the consequences of the crime of 1914? They did not. They were more vigorous than any of the men speakers in demanding a full measure of reprisal on Germany. No one throughout the whole contest whispered "peace."

It was altogether inspiriting. Here was a chance to see what the people of England, the people who stood behind the Army and the Navy and were our ultimate supports, felt about the war. We could see that they were utterly resolute, with not a sign of weariness, nor of fear, nor of tolerance for a craven peace. Their message was "Fight on, Fight on. Bring us home a real peace. We will put up with everything the Boche can do; we will carry on. But no palter, no surrender. Finish the job you are at."

The English people terrorised? Not a bit of it. They were only getting their blood up. And G.H.Q. saw that and was comforted.

There was also a good deal of solid comfort in the way that London took the bitter experience of "rations." We never had any food scarcity in the Army and, going on leave, officer or soldier had a food card that guaranteed him a good holiday supply. So we were in the best position to appreciate the cheerful way in which Great Britain took the very thin gruel of ration times. Every officer coming back from leave expressed his glowing admiration of civilian patience.

Those German agents in London who relieved the tedium of the war for the Allies by reporting to Berlin such "happenings" as the Battle of Oxford Street and the destruction of whole quarters of London by air attacks, set out, for the fooling of the German public, some fine accounts of dismay and discontent caused by food tickets. But as a matter of truth, London on rations surprised and gratified the most cheerful optimists. The old city "took her medicine" not only with patience but with an actual gaiety.

To sum up: between the close of the fighting season of 1917 and the beginning of that of 1918, G.H.Q. was at first a little depressed at the thought that political developments would prevent the Army from seeing the job through in a satisfactory way; was subsequently reassured as to the feeling of the civilian population; and thereafter faced the future with complete confidence.

CHAPTER XVI.

ENTER THE AMERICANS.

How the Germans were misled about the Americans—Early American fighters—The arrivals in May, 1918—American equipment—Our relations with the Americans and what they thought of us—The Portuguese.

THERE are many claimants for the honour of being the War Winner. When I was in Italy in February, 1918, I found a very genuine belief there that the Italians were the genuine war winners; that they brought the decisive weight to bear. Without denying the very useful effect that Italian neutrality had in the first stages of the war, and Italian participation at a later date, I think it would be hard to convince, say, the French of the soundness of the Italian claim. The British might be more inclined to agree; for they still keep up the curious pose of being a poor feckless people who never do anything or know anything. Another claimant for the pride of first place in the Grand Alliance is Greece; and I believe that Portugal has some idea of putting in a claim.

But on the whole, taking all the circumstances into account and reckoning not war services only but war effect, the actual final blow to the Germans' hopes was delivered when the United States of America declared war. It was when Germany made that declaration necessary, in spite of the sincere wish of the Americans to keep out of the war, that all hope vanished of Germany securing an arranged peace. From that moment it was clear that ultimately she would have to take exactly what was handed out to her at the conclusion of the war.

It is hard to believe that the German leaders ever seriously believed the stuff and nonsense that they gave out to comfort their people on the subject of American participation in the war. But having blundered by bringing the United States in they had to try to cover up their blunders.

German diplomacy was not without successes of a kind in the preparation and prosecution of the war. If it is the function of diplomacy to plot murders and strikes and arsons in neutral countries, to bribe Oriental despots such as those of Turkey and Bulgaria into betraying their people, German diplomacy had a proud record. But concerning the sentiments and opinions of honourable communities German diplomacy showed always an abysmal ignorance. In no respect was this more clear than in its dealings with the United States of America.

At first German diplomacy adopted the idea which was embodied in the German phrase "those idiotic Yankees"—the idea that the United States was a kind of Wild West Show, whose simpleton rulers could be fooled without trouble by the intelligent, the super-intelligent, Germans. When that idea was exploded, the next to take its place was equally foolish—that anyhow the antagonism of the United States did not matter, for she would not make war, and if she made war the effort would be so feeble as not to be worth considering.

Then when the grim shadow of the great American preparation was already over the German despotism, and the greatest single white nation of the world was seen preparing its mighty strength to the full, the German people were asked to take comfort from yet another delusion, that the American nation would prove to be a "quitter," that it would be frightened off the field by the German offensive of the Spring of 1918. The *Hamburger Echo* voiced that delusion when it announced: "It is curious that at this critical moment American war experts are reported to be planning an inspection trip of the Front. It looks as though American capitalists were growing nervous. The dollar-republic has stolen ships which ensure her a great Fleet, but American capital is not unlimited, hence the liquidation of the war may be contemplated."

How different the truth about that "inspection trip" which had the effect, certainly, of impressing the American Staff with the extreme seriousness of the campaign, but led to the result not of "quitting" but of brigading the American troops temporarily with those of the Allies. It was an instance of a sensible sacrifice of national vanity that has probably no parallel in history—that decision of the Americans to allow their soldiers to fight under British and French flags while they learned their business.

Unhappy German people to have been fed by their leaders with such delusions! The United States a "quitter"! Had any German read the history of the 18th and 19th centuries—heard of Washington, of Hamilton, of Lincoln? If the German had searched back only so far

ENTER THE AMERICANS.

as 1861 he would have found that the nation which he was told might throw up the sponge at the first hint of hardship and danger, faced a war which probably, for nerve strain and call for grim resolution, surpassed even this great war. The United States had then to fight not a foreign foe but domestic discord. It had to set its teeth through a series of great military disasters. It had to hold firmly to a forlorn hope, whilst it was faced by the ever-present prospect of foreign interference. No nation in modern times has been put to a harsher test of courage and resolution than the United States in 1861 and the following year. No nation in history showed a more indomitable courage. And this was the nation that the German leaders would fain persuade their people was likely to prove a "quitter!" I ventured to say at the time that before the German military despotism was through with the war it would recognise that the reluctance of the United States to enter the war would be matched by the reluctance of the United States to go out of the war until its purpose was finally accomplished.

To tell the story of the American participation in the war does not come within the province of this work, but some of the facts can be told of that most dramatic feature of the last stages of the Great War. There was a very elaborate and very successful mystification of the enemy over the time, the extent, and the equipment of American arrivals on the Western Front. The American "Intelligence," in co-operation with our own and the French Intelligence Branches, managed to surround these matters with so much mystery that some of our own high Staff Officers never knew the exact position, and strangely over-estimated the strength of the American Force on the Western Front. There is good reason to believe that the German High Command was completely deceived and found its difficulties increased accordingly.

From almost the first day of the war there were a few individual Americans fighting for the Allies. In September, 1914, I encountered two personally with the British Army, and I suppose the actual total number was some hundreds. Later a great many came over with the Canadian contingents; and there was also a flying unit, which made a fine reputation for itself. This began with a small group of Americans in the Foreign Legion of the French Army. In the spring of 1915 the formation of an American squadrilla was decided upon. At first the French Minister of War was not inclined to sanction the proposition, but afterwards decided that no international law prevented Americans from enlisting voluntarily, in spite of their country's neutrality. The squadrilla was to be known as the "Escadrille Américaine," and to be commanded by a French captain. On November 16th, 1916, Colonel Barès, Chief of the French Aviation at General Headquarters, decided that the name "Escadrille Américaine" must be dropped and the official military number, N124, used in future. The reason given was that Bernstorff had protested to Washington "that Americans were fighting on the French Front, that the French *communiqués* contained the name 'Escadrille Américaine,' and that these volunteer Americans pushed their brazenness to the point of having a red Sioux Indian in full war-paint depicted on their machines." Captain Berthaud, at the Ministry of War, suggested the adoption of the name "Escadrille de Volontaires," but the name finally adopted was "Lafayette Escadrille." More than 200 American volunteers entered the Lafayette Escadrille before America joined in the war. Some remained in the squadrilla, others were transferred to various French units, where they frequently distinguished themselves by the brilliance of their exploits.

All these troops, however, were strictly unofficial and of course discountenanced by the American Government. After the American declaration of war, American help was confined for a long time to labour units, forestry and railway workers. It was not until May, 1918, that there was any really considerable American fighting force in France, and not until June, 1918, that it began to have any weight in the fighting line, and then only as units brigaded with British and French troops. It was the usual plan—a plan made possible by the admirable and business-like lack of false pride among the Americans—to split up their troops among other troops, allow them thus to be "blooded," and after experience as platoons, companies, brigades, to retire to their own training grounds and form "pukka" Divisions of their own.

By April 25th, 1918, there were 12,700 American troops in our lines in France, by May 25th 79,000, by June 25th 188,000. Then the Second Army Corps was formed and absorbed 95,000 men. The May, 1918, programme provided for the arrival of six American Divisions within the British zone of operations, and there actually were 108,921 American troops attached to the British Army at the end of that month. The British Army took responsibility for the feeding and equipment of these troops. The system was adopted of assigning to each American Division as it arrived a British "mother" Division, to see it through its early troubles of transport, equipment, food and accommodation. The system worked admirably and there was very little friction in connection with the settling down of the Americans. Yet the task of adjustment was not easy. The American troops had to be equipped with almost everything except uniforms, badges and caps. The things they had were almost as much a cause of trouble as the things they had not. The American troops had to be gently separated from huge kits of unnecessary articles at the same time as they were provided with necessities.

Judging from the mountainous kits of the American soldiers as they arrived it was thought that each man carried a roll-top desk, a typewriter, and a dictagraph in his roll. It was found impossible for the men to march with their kits, though they were splendid physical types and full of keenness. I saw one Division disentrain at a station on Lines of Communication and begin a march to its camp, a distance of about ten miles. Before half the distance had been covered a great proportion of the men had had to give up their kits to be stored by the road side.

One American camp was formed at Samer near Montreuil; and the town's name was pronounced near enough to "Sammie" to make it easy to persuade some of the soldiers that it had been named in their honour.

The Americans at first had a natural love for their own methods and their own wonderful kit; but they were very soon convinced of what were the practical needs of the campaign and came in time to a whole-hearted admiration of British methods, which was perhaps the finest testimonial that G.H.Q. could have had. These Americans coming from a great business country confessed quite frankly that the "effete" Britisher had "got them all beat" on questions of supply and transport; and they took over our system in almost every detail. Perhaps some of the points that arose will be of interest. The great underclothing controversy was one of the most amusing. The British Army had evolved a very practical system of keeping the troops in clean under clothing without adding to the weight of their kits. A soldier went up to the trenches or to his unit wearing a clean suit of underclothes. On the first opportunity, usually within a week, the soldier went back (on relief if he were an infantry man, on roster if he were a special unit man) to the Baths which were set up in every Divisional area. Here he stripped for a hot bath, and whilst he was in the bath his uniform was cleaned, deprived of any insect population, and pressed, and his underclothing was taken away to the laundry. He never saw that underclothing again but drew a new suit, or a clean suit, as he went out of the baths; and so he marched off spruce and smart. The suit of underclothing he had left behind was thoroughly disinfected, washed, repaired if necessary, and went then into the general stock to be issued again.

At first the Americans could not see that such a system would work. Their idea was for every man to carry three suits of underclothing, one on his body two in his kit. Presumably he was expected to change in the midst of the ghastly mud of a Flanders trench. Also presumably he was expected to carry about his dirty suits with him, which showed a curious degree of trust in human nature. It was objected to the British system that "all men were not the same size," and in response it was pointed out that neither were all the suits of underclothing kept in stock at Divisional Baths, but that with a fair attention to the law of averages and a reasonable surplus allowance no thin man had to go away with a fat man's suit and no tall man with a short man's. The British system was finally adopted and won full American approval.

Boots caused another difficulty. The British issue was one pair per man; the American, two, the spare pair being carried in the kit. The Americans finally agreed that if they could get for their men boots of British quality (which was conspicuously better than the American quality) the one pair issue would suffice.

It would be impossible to praise too highly the common-sense and civility of the American *liaison* officers who had to argue out these points with our officers. They were never unreasonable, and were very prompt in crediting our officers with politeness and good-will. That Americans and British can get on very well together this campaign has proved. I think that in every case where an American and a British Division were thrown together they parted company with a marked increase of mutual good-will and respect.

Optimism was the prevailing fault in the American organisation. They thought that the fighting was a much simpler matter than it actually proved to be. They thought a man could and would carry an unduly heavy pack. They were very optimistic in the matter of accoutrements and were anxious to use their own accoutrements when they had a barely sufficient supply for the strength of a unit, and no reserve. They were ultimately convinced that accoutrements in warfare have a way of disappearing, and without a strong reserve no item of accoutrement can be kept up. When there was no reserve of some item, British accoutrements were substituted. It is a testimony to the quality of British equipment that the American troops showed a desire to be provided with British articles in substitution for their own, even when the change was not necessary. British puttees and British breeches were cases in point.

The American troops got British rations, except that coffee took the place of tea. One coffee-grinder per 250 men was provided. Perhaps civilian England was puzzled over the fact that in 1918 it was impossible to buy a coffee-grinder in this country. Now they know why. They had all been bought up for the American troops. In all things G.H.Q. did its very best for the Americans. They had a fancy for an increased scale of Machine-Guns; the Machine-Guns were found for them, though they were a precious and scarce commodity at the time and we could not give our own Divisions the increased scale. To provide horse transport for the Americans we stripped our Field Artillery of two horses out of every ammunition team of six. The general principle was that if the Americans wanted anything it had to be found somehow and found in a hurry. Probably we won an undeserved reputation for slickness in some matters (such as printing Army publications), for it was the established rule to give American orders priority.

American *liaison* officers at G.H.Q. "made good" with the British Staff very quickly. They had a downright earnestness of manner which was very engaging. The American Staff seemed to have been chosen strictly for efficiency reasons and, there being no obstacles of established custom to overcome, the best men got to the top very quickly. The appointment of Mr. Frederick Palmer, the famous war correspondent, to a high post on General Pershing's Intelligence Staff was an example of their way of doing things. Colonel Palmer as war correspondent had seen much of this and of many other wars. For his particular post he was an ideal man. But it would be difficult to imagine him stepping at once into so high a position in a European Army. American rank marks were puzzling to British officers at first. An American *liaison* officer obliged me with a mnemonic aid to their understanding.

"You just reckon that you are out to rob a hen-roost. Right. You climb up one bar; that's a lieutenant. You climb up two bars: that's a captain. When you get up to the chickens, that's the colonel" (the colonel's badge was an eagle on the shoulder-straps). "Above the chicken there's the stars" (a star was the badge of a general).

To the same officer I was indebted for a flattering summing up of British character.

"I don't say you British people are over-polite. But you are reliable. Go into a pow-wow and a British officer may strike you as a bit surly. But if he says he'll do a thing you can reckon that thing done and no need to worry. Some other people are very polite; and they say awfully nicely that they'll do anything and everything you ask; and six months after you find nothing has been done."

The Americans, when they got into action, first as auxiliaries of British and French Divisions, then in their own Army organisation, were fine fighters. Their splendid physique made them very deadly in a close tussle, and they had a business-like efficiency in battle that did not appeal to the Boche. A favourite American weapon at close quarters was a shot gun sawn off short at the barrel. It was of fearful effect. The enemy had the sublime impudence to protest against this weapon as "contrary to the usages of civilised warfare." This was cool indeed from the folk who made us familiar with the murder of civil hostages, the use of civilians as fire-screens, and the employment of poison-gas as methods of warfare. The Americans answered the impudent protest with peremptory firmness, and kept the shot gun in use.

It was stated, too, and generally credited, though this matter did not come within my personal observation, that the American Divisions in their sector set up and maintained a law in regard to Machine-Gun fire. They did not consider it fair war that a machine-gunner in an entrenched position should keep on firing to the very last moment and then expect to be allowed to surrender peaceably.

The Americans played the game, but they did not play it on "soft" lines, and the enemy soon got a very wholesome respect for them. There was, in the early stages of the American participation, an evident attempt on the part of the German Intelligence to encourage an "atrocity" campaign against the Americans. German atrocities had a way of casting their shadows before. A usual method was to accuse Germany's foes in advance of doing what the Germans proposed to undertake themselves. That was the way in which Germany ushered in her lawless use of prisoners of war in the firing line, and her enslavement of the civil population of occupied Belgium

ENTER THE AMERICANS.

and France. When the German Press engaged in "propaganda" work on the subject of the American forces coming into action, it took the line of representing the Americans as altogether despicable and murderous adventurers, who had come into the war to kill Germans without any reason whatsoever and when taken prisoners wondered "that they were not shot on the spot, as the French had told them they would be." As one German paper put it: "To the question why America carries on the war against Germany they knew no answer. One can feel for our soldiers who become enraged against this alien hand which fights against us for no reason. Our men believe the French fight for glory and to wipe out the stain of 1870, that Britain struggles for mastery on the sea and to prove which of the two giants is the stronger. But the American! Our field-greys despise him and do not recognise him as a worthy opponent, even though he may fight bravely."

But that sort of talk was soon dropped—as was the suggestion that American prisoners should get "special treatment" when captured. It was rather amusing to watch from our Intelligence side the manœuvres of the well-drilled German Press on the subject of the Americans. Early in 1918 there was a general disposition in the German papers to write of the Americans as tomahawkers and "scalpers" and so on. Then we learned from our tapping of German field reports that officers commanding German units complained that this sort of propaganda was having such a bad effect on their men, that they "got the wind up" as soon as they knew that Americans were in front of them. As a result a great silence suddenly fell upon the German papers on this point.

After the Americans had formed their own Army system we did not hear so much of them at Montreuil. But they were naturally always in close touch with G.H.Q., and to the very end the British Administrative services were able to give a helping hand to the American allies.

The Portuguese contingent remained with the British Army to the end, and it did very well, as might have been expected; for as a race the Portuguese have a proud record of heroism and knightly adventure. In the Indies, the South Pacific, and the Americas, Portuguese valour has left imperishable monuments. The British

Empire in particular owes much to such great sea captains as the Portuguese Vasco di Gama (who discovered the sea route to India), Torres (who discovered and named Australia), Magellan, Quiros, and Menezes.

We heard much amusing gossip at G.H.Q. from the soldiers at the Front, who, after a critical weighing of the facts, arrived at the conclusion that the Portuguese were "good sports." That conclusion was not come to all at once. The British soldier is very conservative, and he was inclined to be, for some reason or other, critical of his new allies at first. In time "Tommy" forgave the Portuguese for having names "that sounded like blooming prayers," which was one of his early reasons for doubt. Here is one incident that helped to determine a favourable verdict:

A forward post held by the Portuguese was subjected to a furious bombardment late one afternoon by the Germans. After a while a polite note came down from the Portuguese officer in charge of the sector informing the British Commander that: "The enemy are heavily bombarding our position. Accordingly we have evacuated it." There was some inclination to criticise; it was not the withdrawal; the best soldiers on earth have to withdraw sometimes. But the polite little note with its "accordingly" suggested what it was not intended to suggest, and what was not the fact at all. However, plans were at once put in hand for artillery action, preparatory to restoring the position next morning. But some time after nightfall those plans were put aside on receipt of another polite little note:

"The enemy has ceased bombarding our position. Accordingly we have re-occupied it."

When the full facts of the incident came out there was a cheer for the Portuguese. It seems that the officer in charge was a bit of a tactician and knew his men well. The post he had to hold was very advanced and poorly fortified. When the enemy began to flood it with shells he withdrew his garrison to a safe spot that he had selected, and waited until nightfall. Then, without any artillery preparation, he led his men forward and, with the bayonet and those deadly little daggers that the Portuguese soldiers carried, restored the position.

An earlier incident of the Portuguese co-operation was humorous in another way. "Tommy" had, of course, found a name for the new arrivals, a name which was more humorous than respectful. Like all Tommy's word-coinages it was a good one and spread into common use. High Authority, fearful that offence would be given, issued an order, a very portentous order, which noticed with reprobation "the habit which had grown up" of referring to "our noble allies" as "the —— ——." The Order concluded with the usual warning of disciplinary action. It was to be circulated secretly by word of mouth from officer to officer, but some unfortunate adjutant circulated it in battalion orders so that all could read—including the Portuguese.

CHAPTER XVII.

THE GERMAN SPRING OF 1918.

Was G.H.Q. at fault?—Where we could best afford to lose ground—Refugees complicate the situation—Stark resolution of the French—All the Pas-de-Calais to be wrecked if necessary—How our railways broke down—Amiens does not fall.

TO affirm that a great German attack was expected in the Spring of 1918, and that the site of the attack was not altogether unexpected, seems to imply a very serious criticism of G.H.Q. That being so, why did the Germans succeed in breaking through and winning such an extent of territory and coming within a narrow margin of gaining a decisive advantage?

The question is natural, especially as one soldier in high command has stated—or is reported to have stated—that he knew exactly the spot where the Germans were going to attack. Some day there will be an exhaustive inquiry into all the circumstances of the Spring of 1918. Probably as a result it will be found that no serious blame can be attached in any quarter, but that what happened was the result of a series of events which were mostly unavoidable.

For the first time Germany could concentrate her whole strength on this Front. Yet our strength was at the lowest point it had reached for many months and, since we had just taken over a new sector of the line, our defence was thinner on the average than it had ever been since 1915. Further, we were definitely short of some essential defence material. If we had strengthened the sector where the chief attack came we should have had to weaken another sector. Then the Germans would have attacked that sector. They chose, and chose naturally, the point where our line was thinnest. If it can be shown that the sector where our line was thinnest was the sector in which we could best afford to lose ground, it will have to be admitted that, in the main, G.H.Q. had made the best dispositions possible with the means at hand.

THE GERMAN SPRING OF 1918.

A glance at the map of France will show that pretty clearly. Put in a phrase, the German plan was to push the British Army into the sea. In the north our line was dangerously close to the sea. Our most northern port, Dunkirk, was actually under shell-fire and in consequence could be very little used. A very small gain of territory by the Germans in the north would have brought Calais and Boulogne under shell-fire. Then our existence as an Army north of the Somme would have become impossible. We could not have kept an adequate force there in supplies. In the north every yard of territory was of the greatest strategic value. As our line ran south the French coast bulged out. We had more room to manœuvre there; loss of ground was not so vital. If the Germans had won on the line Ypres-Armentières the same depth of territory that they won on the line Arras-Péronne, we should have had to evacuate all France north of the Somme.

In short we took the biggest risk of loss of ground where the loss was least dangerous to the vital plan of the campaign. In the light of the man-power available it was probably the best course that could have been pursued. We knew we had to lose ground, probably a good deal of ground, and decided to lose it where it mattered least. We had very good ideas as to where.

For proof of this look up the representations as to civilian evacuations which were made by G.H.Q. to the French authorities in February, 1918. Those representations, by the way, were not given any attention at all in some cases; at the best only perfunctory attention. The result was that when the German attack came, civilian refugees added to our difficulties and anxieties. If the prompt and complete evacuation of all civilian refugees from threatened areas and from areas close behind the front line, which were urgently needed for the accommodation of troops, could have been effected, the Army's tasks would have been much simplified. But that proved impracticable. Civilians were generally unwilling to abandon their homes voluntarily. The French authorities were reluctant to enforce evacuation. A civilian quitting his home voluntarily was responsible for his own keep. A civilian forced to quit became a charge on the French Civil Authorities. This naturally led to a wish that civilians as far as possible should be compelled to quit their homes by force of circumstances rather than by order of the authorities.

As far back as February, 1918, pressure was brought to bear on the French Authorities to agree to defined measures to meet the emergency of a withdrawal of part of our line, which was then foreseen as a probability. But it was not found possible to secure prompt assent to the steps which were necessary. There were all sorts of complications. For one thing it was feared that to set up the machinery of evacuation would spread dismay among the French civilians. Another obstacle was the financial one which I have already mentioned. Yet another was that created by the status of the miners in threatened areas. These were mobilised men under French Military Command; their wives and children were civilians. If their wives and children were evacuated the miners would not stay.

Later, arrangements were agreed to between the British Force and the French Authorities for the systematic evacuation, with their live stock and supplies, of civilians in threatened areas. But the early difficulties considerably hampered operations. I mention this not at all by way of a tilt against the French Authorities, whose reluctance to make provision for evacuations was natural enough, but to show that G.H.Q. was not "caught napping," and to illustrate also the difficulties which an Expeditionary Force operating in a friendly country has to meet.

There are, of course, many advantages springing from the fact that the country in which you are quartered is friendly. But I am not sure that the disadvantages are not almost as great. In an enemy country you know at any rate where you are; military safety, military convenience are the supreme law; and the civilian population have only to be considered to the degree that the laws of war and the dictates of humanity decide. In a friendly country, where the old civil government remains in operation, an Army is hampered at many points. There are various actions which military convenience prompts but which cannot be taken without the assent of the civilian authorities; and perhaps cannot be urged with the weight of the full facts on those civil authorities. This evacuation difficulty is an instance in point. If G.H.Q. had had its way the Germans would have won far less material in their advance; and perhaps their advance would have been stopped at an earlier stage if our operations had not been hampered to some extent by the crowding of the road with civilian refugees.

Still, on the big issues the French were splendid. What, for example, could have been more heroic than the decision they came to a little later: that, in case of the German advance continuing, the whole of the Pas de Calais province was to be destroyed, the harbours

THE GERMAN SPRING OF 1918.

of Dunkirk, Calais and Boulogne wrecked, the dykes and locks destroyed so that the country would have been generally inundated? To some degree defensive inundations were actually carried into effect, but with fresh water only. The responsibility in the main rested with the British Army which was holding the threatened territory. The only saving stipulation made by the French, who thus offered in the cause of the alliance to give up for half a century the use of one of their fairest provinces, was that before the sea was let in to devastate the land, Marshal Foch should give the word. It was on April 12th, 1918, that the Allied Commander-in-Chief gave orders for defensive inundations to stop the Germans from getting to the Dunkirk-Calais region; and on April 13th the Governor of Dunkirk began to put these into effect. There were two schemes of inundation, one for a modified flooding with fresh water of certain limited areas; the other for a general flooding, with sea-water as well as fresh water, of all low-lying areas around Calais and Dunkirk.

It is impossible to praise adequately the stark courage that agreed to this step. It was courage after the antique model, and it showed that France was willing to make any sacrifice rather than allow the wave of German barbarism to sweep over civilisation. The effect of letting the sea in on Pas de Calais and destroying the canal locks and the harbours would have been to make this great province a desert for two generations. The effect of allowing it to fall into German hands, with all its canal and harbour facilities, would have been to give new life to the submarine war, to make the bombardment and ultimately the invasion of the English coast possible.

At one time it seemed almost certain that an evacuation of at least part of Pas de Calais would have to be carried out; and arrangements were made in detail: that in any area which was evacuated, either deliberately or in consequence of direct enemy pressure, the most thorough destruction should be carried out to deny to the enemy any stores of material or facilities of transport. The method of every destruction and the unit responsible for it were arranged in advance.

The main lines of a policy of destruction were laid down in the event of:—

1. A withdrawal to the Calais—St. Omer defensive line;
2. A withdrawal to the line of the Somme;
3. An enemy advance along the line of the Somme, cutting off Flanders and Pas de Calais from the South.

Provision was made for the using up or removal of all possible stores; for the destruction of the remainder; for the destruction of all railroads, water-ways, signalling systems, factories, etc. Where British and French troops were operating together in a fighting zone, their respective responsibilities were delimited. Arrangements were also made, in case of withdrawal, to clear from certain water-ways all canal craft which might serve the enemy as bridge material over inundations.

Certainly it was not "gay," as the French say, this preparation for destroying the property of an Ally. But we took comfort from the fact that after all the position was better than in 1914. Then a German victory seemed possible. Now in 1918 the only question was what sacrifices we should yet have to make before achieving victory. In 1914, after 50 years of intensive preparation, the German had rushed upon an unsuspecting Europe. He neglected nothing in preparing for victory. He threw overboard every scruple in order to secure a rapid triumph, violating the neutrality of Belgium and Luxemburg merely because by so doing he gained a better field of deployment. His objective was Paris, and, according to authoritative accounts, his plan on reaching Paris was to divide it up into twelve quarters and burn down a quarter every day that the French Army delayed to surrender. The terms of surrender were to include the giving up of the French Fleet and the French ports for use in an invasion of England.

The danger at that time was very real. Germany was the only country adequately armed and organised. The British people had had to sacrifice in great measure the Regular Army to stay the first German onset. France was strained to a point which to any other country would have meant exhaustion. We could recall the preparations that had to be made to meet the imminent fear of an invasion of the British coast; the desperate shifts and expedients which had to be adopted in the first stages of the organisation of the New Armies; the peremptory demands for guns and shells when there were no factories to make either in anything like the quantity demanded. That was a time when it needed the highest of moral courage to remain calm and confident. The Spring of 1918 is not a pleasant thing to think about; but it is hardly endurable, even now in safe retrospection, to think on the position of Great Britain at home or in the field from October, 1914, to September, 1915. It was that of an unsuspecting man before whose feet suddenly a pit of destruction opens. He falls scrambling, struggling down, and at last reaches a little ledge which gives a momentary safety. But it is still a desperate task merely to hang on. Far up, remote almost as a star, shines safety. Below are his friends of civilised Europe, all worse situated than himself, some at the point of complete destruction. From above a fierce storm of missiles rains on his head. From below come piteous appeals for help. To hold on to his little ledge, to help the friends below, to climb up and throttle the foe above—he has all these to do and little time to think before he acts. Hardly endurable, yet necessary to think over, so that the greatness of the danger into which the world was plunged by German militarism can be gauged.

In 1914 an occupation of the French Channel Ports with England almost entirely unarmed might have been a very serious thing. The serious view taken of it in Great Britain can be judged from the preparations which were made to devastate a great area in the South and East of England so as to give to the Germans only a desert as a foothold. In 1918 if the Germans had got Pas de Calais they would not have got any ports with it, and an invading force arriving in England would have met a force at least equal to it in equipment and war experience.

So we waited in some confidence for another Marne to follow another Mons, and smiled a little grimly at the change of tone in Germany. The Kaiser, cock-a-whoop again, was declaring now for a "strong German Peace." In one office, side by side with the "situation map" which showed from day to day the depth of the German advance, there were stuck up in derision extracts from the most vituperative of the German press. Here is one from the *Deutsche Zeitung*:

"Away with all petty whining over an agreement and reconciliation with the fetish of peace.... Away with the miserable whimpering of those people who even now would prevent the righteous German hatred of England and sound German vengeance. The cry of victory and retaliation rages throughout Germany with renewed passion."

This from *Germania*:

"There can be no lasting peace and no long period of quiet in the world until the presumptuous notion that the Anglo-Saxons are the chosen people is victorious or defeated. We are determined to force with the sword the peace which our adversaries did not see fit to confide to our honest word. We Germans are an incomparably strong nation."

These horrible threats remained on the notice-board until long after the tide of battle turned and the German was in full retreat back to his lair.

And we rather liked the story which the German press had to the effect that a deputation of German business men had put before Hindenburg in February the gloomy prospects of the country's food supplies, concluding: "In May, Germany will be almost without food." Hindenburg thereupon replied: "My reply is that I shall be in Paris on April 1st."

The date chosen seemed so appropriate!

Still, it would be foolish to say that we had no anxieties. Some of our stoutest fellows were up at "advanced G.H.Q.," a temporary H.Q. near Amiens, from which most of the really exciting work was done. At Montreuil we had not the exhilarating feeling of being within the sound of the guns, but had to face perhaps the hardest of the toil. It was rare for an officer in some branches to leave his room before midnight, and the usual hour for starting work was 8.30 a.m. Meals ceased for a time to be convivial affairs. One rushed to the table, ate, and rushed back to work.

The work was so overwhelming because of a combination of circumstances. The character of the War had changed from stationary to moving over almost all the British Front, calling for a return to the mobile system of supply and for new classes of material. British reinforcements were arriving from other Fronts, sometimes without their full supply train and without the full equipment for our Front, and not familiar with its system of working. There were large movements of French troops into British Areas, and in some cases these French troops relied upon British sources for some of their supplies and transport, and in all cases their line of supply had to be dove-tailed in with ours. American troops were moved into British Areas and relied upon British sources for many items of equipment, transport and supplies. British Administration was thus being called upon for supplies to British, French, American and Portuguese troops, at the same time as our lines of supply had to be re-organised and co-ordinated with the new French lines of supply. Further difficulties were created by the necessary frequent changes of railheads and the great movements on the roads of civilian refugees. Territory threatened by the enemy had to be evacuated as far as possible of civilians, and of civilian goods and stock likely to be of use to the enemy in case of capture.

THE GERMAN SPRING OF 1918.

The extent of this accumulated difficulty from a transport point of view can be gauged from the fact that a British Army needs on a day of intense fighting 1,934 tons of supplies of all kinds *per mile of front.*

The railways came as nearly as possible to a complete breakdown under the strain. After the first Battle of the Somme, our military railway system in France was thoroughly reorganised by civilian experts. It was a reorganisation which followed, I believe, the best models of the great railway companies of England, and it coped with the very heavy traffic during the period of fixed or Trench War quite well. Unfortunately it was not a system adapted for moving warfare.

A civilian railway expert would doubtless find many reasons for amused criticism in a military railway system in the running. It would appear to be rather haphazard, to be run a good deal on the principle of a train getting there if it could, and to be very faulty in the matter of time-tables and so on. Well, the German advance in its brutal practical way simply riddled with holes that admirable railway reorganisation which the civilian experts had conferred on the B.E.F., France.

Perhaps it was only to have been expected. Trench War in its railway requirements was deceptively like peace. You had your railway termini, and the requirements of a Division were fairly stable. You ran so many trains a day and, except for an occasional rush on some sector when fighting warmed up suddenly, there were no problems that differed greatly from those say of the London, Brighton and South Coast Railway.

In moving war it is different. Then a railway system must be elastic enough to stand such a series of shocks as would be conveyed to the L.B. and S.C. manager if at 9 p.m. he were told: "It is Bank Holiday to-morrow. Provide for carrying 100,000 extra passengers, about 10,000 horses and 4,000 carriages." Then at 10 p.m. he learned: "You can't shunt any trains at Lewes; and you can only run trains through with luck. It is under heavy shell-fire." Then every half-hour subsequently he got a new order, diverting traffic from one point to another, changing the destinations of his trains and so on.

The transport situation for the moment was saved by the Motor Transport. But the Commander-in-Chief had to act promptly and set up a "jury-mast" arrangement for railway control to tide over the crisis. In effect he took the supreme control of the railways out of the hands of the Transportation Directorate and put it under a "Board of Directors" meeting daily, at which the Q.M.G. presided. A later development made the Chief of General Staff Chairman of this Board. Then, when things settled down, the system that had been set up by the civilian experts was largely scrapped. Military Railways were again put under the control of the Quartermaster-General. The "stupid soldiery" did rather well with them, not only in the period of pause that came between the German advance and our great counter-attack, but in the gigantic task of following up our advance.

The task of pulling together the railways was not an easy one. The enemy advance had caused a direct loss of some light railway systems, and on the broad-gauge systems important engine depôts were lost, and our front lateral line was brought at several points under the fire of the enemy's artillery. Use of this front lateral line had thus become precarious. The results of this were felt in every part of the railway system. Good circulation is the essence of railway working; and a block at any point has an effect similar to that of an aneurism on a human artery. Because of the loss of engine depôts, and the hindrances to circulation on the front lateral line, the back lateral line along the coast became seriously congested. This congestion reduced the capacity of every engine by an average of 15 per cent.

Further, our rear lateral line had two particularly vulnerable points, one at Etaples, where it crossed the Canche, and the other at Abbéville, where it crossed the Somme. Upon these points enemy aircraft made frequent attacks, imposing delays, occasionally causing minor destruction, always adding to the effects of the existing congestion. An excellent piece of work reduced very considerably the effect of one successful enemy air-raid. Half an hour after midnight, one night in May, the Canche railway-bridge at Etaples was damaged. At once an avoiding line—constructed for such an emergency—was put into operation, and trains were running through at 2 a.m.

On one of the worst nights of the German advance, when we went up to the situation-map without any enthusiasm, half afraid of what we should see, young Captain Hannibal Napoleon deepened our gloom by declaring oracularly:

"If we hold on to Amiens we shall be all right. If Amiens falls to the Germans it is goodbye to Montreuil, and no more Paris leave for a few years."

Hannibal Napoleon (that, of course, was not his name) was very junior and very confident of his strategical genius. It was a favourite amusement to "pull his leg" and draw from him an "appreciation" of the situation, which he was always willing to give with the authority of a Commander-in-Chief.

This oracle was displeasing, because on the appearance of things that night we had not an earthly chance of holding Amiens. But the unexpected happened. Not very many hours afterwards the news came through that a successful stand was being made in front of Amiens; and young Hannibal Napoleon was able to crow like a Gallic cock over his profound strategical judgment.

CHAPTER XVIII.

THE MOTOR LORRY THAT WAITED.

How a motor lorry waited at the Ecole Militaire to take away the maps to the Coast—The Motor Lorry Reserve—An "appreciation" of the position—Germany lost the War in the first three months—Some notes of German blunders.

ONE night in the Spring of 1918 a mysterious motor lorry drew up in the yard of the Ecole Militaire at Montreuil. Its driver reported and was ordered to stand by. He stood by all that night; and in the morning was relieved by another driver. But the empty lorry still waited. At night a relief driver came on duty. But the empty lorry still waited.

THE MOTOR LORRY THAT WAITED.

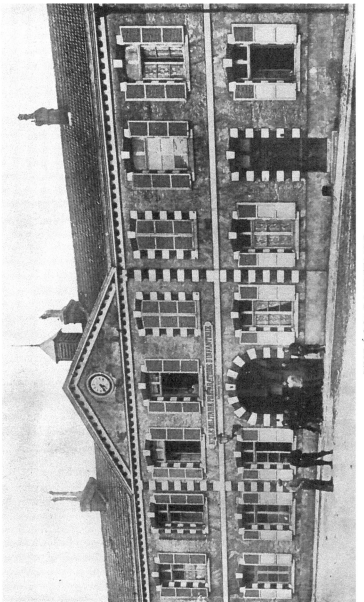

THE ÉCOLE MILITAIRE

G. H. Q. (MONTREUIL-SUR-MER)

Lorries in those days were precious. Because the German had seized many of our light railways, had put under his shell-fire our main front lateral line and had brought our whole railway system to a point perilously close to collapse, the fate of the British Army was to a great extent dependent on its motor lorries. By an intuitional stroke of genius, or of luck, the new Quartermaster-General had just brought to completion one of his "gyms"—the building up of a G.H.Q. reserve of motor lorries. There had been all kinds of explanations of that reserve—mostly of the humorous-malicious order. It had been said that they were intended to carry about the baggage of the G.H.Q. Generals; that the reserve had no other reason for being than to find a soft job for some potentate near to the golf links of the coast. But whether it was just a guess or a bit of far-seeing on the part of Sir Travers Clarke, that G.H.Q. Motor Lorry Reserve had been built up; and it was available to rush into the breach when the railways could not face the task of supply.

Very nobly the Motor Transport—including that reserve—did its duty. There were drivers who held the wheel for thirty-six hours at a stretch, and were lifted from their seats fainting or asleep; a few—who carried on until no longer able to see through their bloodshot and torturing eyes—ran their cars into trees or walls or ditches. There were many casualties, but the situation was saved.

It was just at this time, when a motor lorry was above rubies in value, that an entirely healthy, well-preserved example, with driver attached, was ordered to remain in the yard of the Ecole Militaire.

Everyone wanted to know the reason why. The position was then at its very worst, so the humourist who surmised that it was "waiting for the wine orders of the —— Mess," for once found his jape fall flat. The truth was for a long time known only to a select few. That motor lorry was told off to carry away the maps and important papers from Montreuil to the coast, since the evacuation of the town and of all France north of the Somme was possible at an hour's notice.

So critical was the position for some days that that motor lorry was never off duty night or day.

But G.H.Q. went about its work unperturbed to all outward seeming, and there was not a whisper of losing the war, not even from those who knew what would be the full consequences of evacuating Pas de Calais. One officer—he would not like his name to be published even now—spoke with the most frank recognition of facts and yet with a robust confidence that was distinctly comforting:

THE MOTOR LORRY THAT WAITED.

"If we go behind the Somme it will give the Germans the Coast from the Canche right up to the Scheldt for their submarines. That is the most serious factor. We won't leave them much in the way of harbour works, of course; but still they will be able in a year or two to restore things a bit."

"In a year or two? But will it last...?"

"Oh yes, you can give the war another ten years at least in that event. For there won't be any American Army to speak of; no port to land them or supply them from. Our British Army will have to come down in strength for the same reason. You can't keep a bigger army anywhere than you can keep supplied with food and shells. Look at the ports and the railways. There will be Havre, Brest, Cherbourg, Bordeaux as ports of supply and the railways from them as the channels of supply to the front line. No good talking of millions of Americans pouring in. They can't pour. Funnel's too narrow."

But there wasn't in that officer's mind a hint of the possibility of failure.

"It's only a question of organising to get at them. In time weight must tell. The Germans and their friends are, say, 140,000,000 in population. The allies who are in the war against them have 600,000,000 of population and another 400,000,000 of reserve population if Japan came in fully, and China, and Brazil. I count Russia on neither side, but she is still a liability more than an asset to the Germans. In money and resources the odds against them are even greater. I like to go back to the simple basis of arithmetic sometimes. Of course weight doesn't tell against skill. But now the skill is about even. The Germans had their one and only chance at the beginning, the very beginning, of the war; because they were ready and no one else was. They had to win by Christmas, 1914, or not to win at all."

He went on to sketch vividly the story of the war up to that date, the very nadir of our depression. He argued that the enemy had obviously committed some tremendous blunders. The Prussian military leaders had been very clever in securing spectacular victories (generally after a preliminary corruption of some weak section of their opponents) and thus the military position was not easy to see in its true proportion. But even a surface consideration must show that whilst Germany was always announcing victories, she was never really within sight of victory.

"In the first instance the Prussian Empire had made no sound reckoning of the forces she had to meet. That was the first elementary duty of the strategist. The man who goes out to fight ten thousand and finds he has to fight twenty thousand has blundered irreparably. In 1914 Prussia calculated that Great Britain would not participate in the war, and would consent not only to the destruction of France but to the betrayal of her obligations towards Belgium. The bewildered dismay with which Germany learned that Great Britain would not look upon the treaty with Belgium as a 'scrap of paper,' the wild hatred toward England which found one expression in the 'Hymn of Hate,' were the screams of a savage creature caught in a trap.

"She had then one slender chance, a rush attack on Paris. But the Battle of the Marne killed that chance. Then the only hope of saving Germany was to make peace. But she had made the ghastly blunder of the Belgian atrocities.

"When a man goes out to fight ten thousand and finds himself confronted by twenty thousand it is common prudence to strive to make the stakes as low as possible, the penalty of failure as small as possible. There was a chance that, if that policy had been followed, the war would have come to an end soon after the Battle of the Marne, an end not favourable to Prussian ideas of European domination, giving those ideas a severe check, but still not wrecking them irrevocably nor exacting a very heavy penalty. But the Prussian spirit added blunder to blunder. Having launched a hopeless war it set itself to give that war an 'unlimited' character. Instead of going through Belgium as a reluctant trespasser, the Prussian army trampled through as a ravaging devastator in full blast of frightfulness. By the time Prussia had fought and lost the Battle of the Marne she had steeled her enemies to an inflexible resolution against a compromise peace."

Prussia, he argued, thus early by two blunders of the first magnitude (1) entered into a campaign against an alliance which ultimately could command vastly superior forces, and (2) embittered the conditions of the campaign so that her withdrawal from it was made exceedingly difficult. Several blunders of a lesser order marked the first stages of the campaign. Belgium having been attacked and Liége taken, the Prussian army showed a strange hesitancy and lack of enterprise when faced by the little Belgian army on the line Haelen-Tirlemont-Namur. Precious days were lost in pottering. Whether it was expected that the Belgian nation would give way after one defeat, or it was thought that French and British armies had been pushed up into Belgium, the German millions were held up an unduly long time by the Belgian thousands.

THE MOTOR LORRY THAT WAITED.

At Mons the German Army neither crushed the French-British force nor pushed it back so quickly that the main deployment was harassed. Whether this failure of the German Army was due to its bad handling or to the excellent virtues of the French-British force, did not matter. But the Battle of Mons frustrated the only hope that was left to Germany at that time—a successful rush on Paris opening the way to a quick peace. It proved that there was no military genius at the head of the German invaders. Then the Army which had been delayed in Belgium was defeated on the Marne and had to fall back on the Aisne. The explanation for this given in some German quarters was that the Army had outstripped its big guns and ammunition supplies. That was as good as any other. No explanation would clear the Prussian Military Command from the stigma that it failed when there was that one remaining desperate chance of success.

And having failed on the Marne and retreated to the Aisne the German strategic plan lost all coherency. True, the war was lost so far as any hope of winning European dominancy was concerned. But there was still as a possible objective a peace which would secure Prussia something in return for the territory which she had overrun. Such a peace had been made difficult by the cold rage inspired by Prussian frightfulness. But it was the only possible aim left and, from a military point of view, it could only be pursued in one way, by a definite hammering at some vital point to secure a decisive result, with a defensive stand in other quarters. A defensive campaign in the East with a determined offensive in the West, or a defensive on the West with a resolute offensive on the East.

The Prussian vacillated between the two; his effort was always shuttlecocking East to West, West to East, getting a decisive result nowhere. Like a baited bull in the arena Prussia was constantly making sensational rushes here and there, gratified often by the sight of fleeing foes, but never breaking out of the arena of doom, and always losing blood.

"The first three months of the war," he concluded dogmatically, "were decisive. They do not redound to the military glory of Prussia. During those three months the disciplined and trained devotion of the German troops worked wonders in the battle line. But indecision at Headquarters prevented the proper concentration of their efforts. Prussia had failed to conquer Europe unprepared. She was afterwards face to face with the task of conquering Europe prepared; and her indecision increased. She was always looking for success in a new quarter and never finding it. Recklessness and vacillation and impatience are not sound military qualities, but they mark the whole military history of Germany since November, 1914. Recklessness of ultimate consequences was shown in such matters as the bringing of poison gas into use. Vacillation was shown by the effort which was organised to take the French Channel ports at all costs, and, failing, was diverted to the Eastern Front, and back again to this Front, and then again to the Balkan Front, and back to this Front and then to the Italian Front and finally back to this Front. Impatience was shown in the general failure to push any effort to its logical conclusion, and in details, such as the haste with which poison gas was put into use on a small and ineffectual scale instead of being kept in reserve for a great and possibly decisive effort."

"Take it year by year," this officer concluded, "it has been always the same. Germany has added always to the area of destruction. She has never got nearer to victory. It will be the same with this Push. If that motor lorry has to carry away the maps from Montreuil it may be another ten years before we beat the Germans, but we will beat them."
"But if France gives in?"
"France won't give in. Look at her now, ready to smash up all Pas de Calais—to blow up every harbour and canal and road. That does not look like giving in. Even if she were forced to it we could go back to our island and carry on the fight from there."

Then we talked of lighter things.
Going out from dinner my friend reverted to the war position.
"Anyhow that lorry is not going to take the maps. I bet you a cigar to nothing."

He was right. Going up to the map room on the Intelligence side we heard that our troops were holding in front of Amiens. We had actually passed the lowest point of our fortunes, and within a week the motor lorry had gone.

I asked one of the drivers detailed to it, who either did not know or wisely professed not to know what he had been kept in waiting for, what he thought about it all. He replied with that sound philosophy of the British soldier:
"It was a splendid 'mike,' Sir."
"Mike," it need hardly be explained, is a trade term in the Army for a soft job.

CHAPTER XIX.

THE UNITY OF COMMAND.

Was it necessary?—Was a French Generalissimo inevitable?—Our share in the guiding of the last phase of the campaign—Points on which the British had their way.

THE "unity of command" achieved in the Spring of 1918 caused hardly a ripple of comment at G.H.Q. Some days after it had happened we learned that Lord Milner (then Secretary of State for War) had been over, and that, with the approval of Lord Haig, Field Marshal Foch had become Commander-in-Chief of the Allied Armies.

I suppose that in their secret hearts many officers felt a little sad that the honour of the united command had not fallen to a British General. But there was no question as to the wisdom of the choice nor as to the wisdom of the step itself. It was one of the early misfortunes of the campaign that the British Government in 1914 had insisted very strongly on keeping our Army as an absolutely independent unit in France. The reasons, one may presume, were political rather than strategical; and that there was still some remnant of the old prejudice against "continental entanglements." I do not suppose that if the issue had been left to the soldiers themselves there would have been any doubt but that the small auxiliary British Force would have "reported to" the main French Army and acted under its direction. That would have been the natural military course. But the position became more difficult as the importance of the British Army grew. At the time that the united Command was achieved the British Army was in fighting force an equal unit to the French.

Two questions are often raised in connection with this decision of 1918: Was it necessary? Was it inevitable that the united command should go to Marshal Foch? Both questions may be answered with "yes;" though in each case the "yes" needs to be qualified with some explanation.

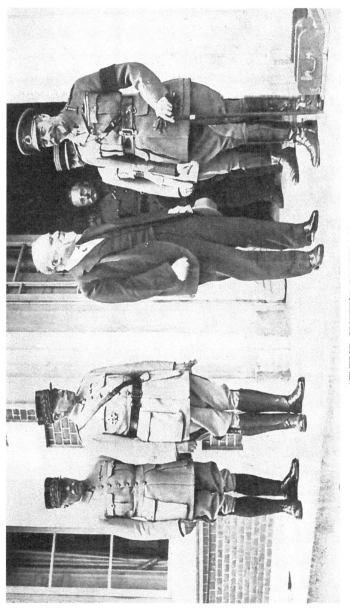

AT THE CHIEF'S CHATEAU

THE UNITY OF COMMAND.

It is, for instance, hardly correct to say that the decision to unite the command "won the war;" though it is probably correct that it hastened the date of victory. Before it was achieved there was good co-operation, though not perfect co-operation, between the Allied Forces. After it was achieved there was maintained a certain independence of outlook and of policy on the part of the British Command which was a great factor in the speedy consummation of victory. If that independence had not been maintained, the operations of 1918 would, almost certainly, not have been so gloriously decisive. This aspect of the final campaign has never been discussed to my knowledge, yet a knowledge of it is important if the events of 1918 are to be viewed in their proper perspective.

I suppose the average "man in the street" takes the view that early in 1918, the British Army, which had been blundering along up till then, was put under French Command and straightway the war was won. But it was not at all like that. The British Army command, whilst giving the most loyal support to the French Generalissimo and bowing to his decisions when they were finally made, read it as its duty still to keep a share in the conduct of the campaign; and in many most important conclusions it upheld its own view as against the French view. The final result in some matters showed that the British view was the right view, and that if it had not been taken the victorious advance would not have been possible.

In an earlier chapter I have given the facts about the forage ration. It was not exactly a matter of the first importance, some may say. But if the French view had been accepted and the British and American horse ration had come down to the French level our horse transport would not have been able to carry on as wonderfully as it did from August to November, 1918. As things were, it had nothing to spare during the last week, as our pursuing troops can tell. The French with their logical minds argued that if their horses could do with a certain ration, ours could. In this case the apparently logical conclusion was not the sound one; for it left out of consideration some factors—as to whether we did not use our horses more, and as to whether our men could get, or would try to get, the same work out of ill-fed horses. In this matter it was well for the Allied cause that the British had their way.

In another matter logic threatened to lead to a step which might have proved disastrous. The French saw, as the logical corollary of the united command, a union, a pooling of all the supply and transport departments. Not only should the Armies fight under one strategical direction but they should share and share alike all their resources. A decision to this effect was actually come to, the Americans agreeing with the French view. It was logical without a shadow of doubt. But British common-sense recognised that if this radical reorganisation were attempted in 1918 it would be 1920 before the Alliance would have been ready for a great Push. The British Army—let it be confessed with appropriate candour and shamefacedness—was much more exigent in its demands than the French. It needed, or thought it needed, more food, more clothing, more comforts, more ammunition, more transport. It had evolved for itself during the campaign a system of "housekeeping" which was over-liberal, perhaps, as compared with the French, but which was mainly a result of the generosity of the Home people, and was so deeply rooted in our Army organisation that to have torn it up in 1918 would have caused all kinds of trouble.

In June, 1918, the "Executive Inter-Allied Committee on Supply" was formed by an agreement between the French and the American governments, to which the British government at first (apparently) assented. It was to take over control of all Supply, Storage, and Transport, and to have executive functions, *i.e.*, its decisions would be binding on all the Armies. The British Command at once saw that this was impracticable—that it was impossible in the very midst of the preparations for the Great Push to throw into a common pool so much of the actual equipment of the Army. The Allied Command was very stubborn in supporting its plan. But in time British common-sense proved stronger than abstract logic, and in July all was made happy by a decision that the functions of the Board were to *advise* on matters of Supply and Storage and methods of utilising material, as far as practicable, for the common benefit of the Allies. The Board, in short, was to have its scope in assisting to maintain the excellent understanding which already existed between the Armies of the Allies in regard to Supplies and Services.

The position was not at all that the British Army wanted to wallow in luxury whilst its Allies went short, for it was always willing to help in every possible way; but that its command knew that the essentially national system of "housekeeping" which had been set up, could not be thrown down at an hour's notice without grave danger.

The same sort of problem was always cropping up on a smaller scale in areas where French troops were fighting with the British. The French had at first a logical aspiration for an identity of supply systems.

THE UNITY OF COMMAND.

Our view was that when British and French troops were operating together, it was not possible to serve both from a common stock, nor by a common railway service. Ammunition and Supplies differed in almost every respect, and the systems of Supply could not be identical. Except in regard to a few items, one Army could not supply the other satisfactorily. Therefore, each Army should have its own depôts, railheads, and—for the sorting of supplies—its own regulating stations, which would receive from Base full trains loaded with particular items of supply and send out to Divisions full trains loaded with the necessary assortments of different items. Something could be done in the way of pooling bulk stores, such as forage, coal, and petrol; but for most things there must be different channels of supply.

British policy was that a British Force in a French area should provide completely for its own maintenance, and organise its supply lines and depôts accordingly. Ultimately it was recognised on both sides that this was the only possible policy, and that the trouble of providing separate regulating stations, separate railheads, and depôts must be faced. Any half-way policy was seen to be fraught with too many possibilities of dangerous failures.

To cite yet one more instance of the British policy proving the sounder: In July, 1918, there were very strong indications that the German power of offensive had passed its zenith and that the enemy might be forced shortly to a great withdrawal. There was set on foot in the British Army at the earliest opportunity an examination of the measures of Transport and Supply which would become necessary if the Germans were forced to withdraw their line. In 1916-1917 the enemy had been able to avoid, to a great extent, the consequences of his defeats on the Somme and the Ancre by retiring his line; a promptly effective pursuit was hindered by lack of the necessary material on our part. A foreseeing preparation would enable a better harvest of victory to be reaped if the position of 1916-1917 were reproduced in 1918. We wanted to be sure of being able to follow up with about 2,000 tons of supplies per day per mile of front to carry our troops over the Hindenburg Line.

There was found to be a divergence of view as to the best means of following up. The French were inclined to put their faith chiefly in light railways. The British idea was that light railways could be overdone; that there was not a full appreciation of the modification in the rôle of the light railway consequent on the change from trench to moving warfare; that there was a tendency for light railways to attempt to duplicate the work of broad-gauge railways; and a hint of a tendency to look upon light railways as a substitute for, instead of a reinforcement of, roads in the forward area.

The British "pursuit policy," to put it briefly, was to concentrate all available labour on pushing forward with the broad-gauge railways and the roads forward from them, trusting to motor transport and to horse transport to pick up the burden from broad-gauge railhead. This was maintained to be a superior policy to concentrating on light railways, which could not allow so much freedom in lines of advance. The British view prevailed in our sector, and in the Great Pursuit it proved to be sound. The Germans were followed up on our sector of the Front in really fine fashion. In the Somme sector of the Front between August 8th and September 8th our broad-gauge railheads were pushed forward an average of 30 miles. To these new railheads, all kinds of traffic could go direct from the Base to meet there our Motor Transport (and, of course, light railways; these were not neglected but given secondary importance).

It was at first the French idea to "sandwich" the various Divisions of the two Armies, to have a British Division or Corps side by side with a French wherever possible. This again would have been a beautifully logical illustration of the complete identity and fraternity of the two armies, but it was not business. It multiplied difficulties of administration, and it was finally abandoned, much to the advantage of the common cause.

These matters I cite not with the idea of deprecating the French General Staff—there were presumably as many instances in which their view was right and ours was wrong—but to show that it is not fair to our G.H.Q. to assume, as many do assume, that the British High Command had little or nothing to do with the planning of the great victory. Marshal Foch is prompt to resent that view when it is obtruded. He would, without a doubt, agree that the British were most loyal in service, and also very independent and stubborn (and often prevailing) in council. Probably looking back upon the great victory which was won under his *bâton* he is profoundly grateful that the British were so forthright in helping to keep the Allied operations on the best track.

The other question, asked at the beginning of this chapter, needs to be explained. Was it inevitable that Marshal Foch should be chosen as Generalissimo? It is quite certain that no other choice was possible in view of all the circumstances. There is no need to come to the question of who was the more renowned soldier, or to argue that if Lord Haig had been given the same chance he would probably have achieved the same result. Personally I think that the British Army in 1918 was in respect of Generalship as in other respects equal to any in the Field. But that was not the issue. We were fighting on French soil and had to demand great sacrifices from the French civilian population, which a French Generalissimo could best get. It was quite certain that the British Army would fight with exactly the same enthusiasm under a French Generalissimo; it was not possible to be so certain that the French Army would under a British Generalissimo.

There was no contested election for the post. Lord Haig as well as General Pershing supported Marshal Foch's claims. It was the work and not the glory of the work which was the first consideration.

"SOMEWHERE IN FRANCE"

CHAPTER XX.

THE COMING OF VICTORY.

The June Position—German attempts to pinch out our lines of supplies—The attacks on hospitals—The glorious last 14 weeks—G.H.Q.'s share.

BY June, 1918, it was fairly evident that the German attack to drive the British to the sea had exhausted itself. The enemy had attempted to push through along the Somme line, separating the British and the French Armies. Foiled in that by the stubborn defence in front of Amiens, he tried a push towards the Channel ports, which really gave more anxiety at G.H.Q. than the earlier move, for there we were working on such a very narrow margin of safety that every yard lost was a grave peril.

The final effort of the enemy was to pinch us out of territory which he could not push us out of, and this effort, though it led to no great battles, was a very serious menace. During the month of June there was not a day's respite from the pertinacious efforts of the enemy to strangle our arteries of supply. Having arrived, at some places, within range of our front lateral railway line, the enemy sought by continuous bombardments to stop or at least hamper traffic, at the same time constantly attacking with aircraft our rear lateral railway line at its most sensitive points, the Somme and the Canche crossings. The ports of entry and the supply depôts were also repeatedly attacked. Inconvenience—serious at times—and loss followed from these attacks, but there was never an actual stoppage of essential traffic.

Provision had been made to prevent any blows that the enemy was able to deliver being really effective Alternative avoiding lines took up promptly the task of broken channels of traffic, and strenuous work in repair and good emergency organisation prevented congestion ever reaching the stage of paralysis. At one time during this month it was necessary to stop for a few days all but absolutely essential traffic from North to South. That was the limit of the enemy's success, though he was aided in some degree by an influenza epidemic (which sadly reduced the supply of labour for railway and dock work).

One line of German tactics at this time was rather "over the edge" as Tommy put it. That was to attack the Base hospitals by aircraft. One at Etaples was set on fire and destroyed. There is, I admit, some room for a shadow of a doubt as to whether the German deliberately attacked the hospitals or only accidentally. That shadow of a doubt must be granted, because it was a fact that several of our hospitals were near to large railway junctions and camps, though always clearly marked and separated from other military installations. I am not prepared to question the good faith of those who give the Germans the benefit of the doubt, though I cannot agree with them. The attacks on the hospitals came in June, just when the Germans concentrated their strategy on trying to cripple our means of supply. They inflicted grave embarrassment on our resources, for, at a time when material was very short and lines of transport fearfully congested, we had to construct new hospitals and move patients and staffs. A note made in July on the point reads:

"Good progress is being made with the transfer to other areas of hospitals which were rendered necessary by enemy aircraft attacks. Though there is very little doubt possible that the enemy does not intend to respect hospitals, wherever they may be sited, in his bombing raids, the precaution is being taken of choosing new hospital sites well away from any point of military importance. No hospital will be established near military camps, important railway junctions, or bridges."

If it was by a series of accidents that the Germans succeeded in hitting a number of hospitals in June, 1918, they were singularly fruitful accidents for him. The difference, from a "results" point of view, in bombing a camp and a hospital is this: if you bomb a camp you kill a few men but the camp does not move; if you bomb a hospital you kill a few patients, nurses, and doctors, and you force the hospital to move, if it can move, to an apparently safer place.

In June there was cause for anxiety in the whole supply position. Seeing that the existence of the armies depended on maintaining to the full the huge rate of supply which modern war demands, and that the

THE COMING OF VICTORY.

enemy was obviously trying immediately behind our lines the policy (which was exactly the same as the policy of his submarine campaign) of pinching out lines of supply, it was judicious to try to extend the margin of safety. One way of effecting this which was explored was to extend "Lines of Communication" to England, and to keep in England at places handy for shipment to France one half the reserve stores of the Army. In most items the Army worked on a month's reserve margin. The storing of this month's reserve in the comparatively narrow strip of France which we held, subject to constant bombing, was becoming a matter of extreme difficulty. The retreat of the Germans began, however, before any definite steps in the direction of setting up reserve stores on the coast of England were taken.

There was no idea that the enemy was going to collapse so suddenly. G.H.Q. expected to drive him back to the Hindenburg line in 1918 and to finish him off in 1919. In the middle of July, 1918, the matter was before the General Staff with the discussion of plans founded on the postulate that the Germans might withdraw to the Hindenburg line, and that a prompt following up in full force was intended. An instruction to the Director General of Transportation asked for facts as to new railway material that would be needed in such a contingency. The problem of effective pursuit, it was recognised, would be largely one of Supplies and Transport. If our Army could be brought up to the new German line promptly, and maintained there with all the means of vigorous attack, all kinds of pleasant results might be hoped for. But nobody really was so optimistic as to think that the enemy would throw in his hand before the winter. But we prepared for the best as well as for the worst.

The task of getting ready to put Pas de Calais in ruins in case of a German advance was pleasantly interrupted by the now more urgent task of getting ready to follow up the enemy with horse, foot, artillery, and with some scores of thousand of tons of supplies daily. The fruits of this were reaped in August, when all agreed that the troops had been well followed up. Cases of real hardships were very rare. Some admirably prompt work was done in railway construction, road restoration, and canal clearing. One great main road was opened to traffic two hours after its capture. Traffic on the Albert line was restored to Corbie and Heilly the day after capture. The water supply difficulty was great, and in many cases water for both men and horses had to be sent up by motor and pack transport. But on the territory won our old water bores were found in most cases intact, and were promptly restored to usefulness by the R.E. Baths and laundries followed in close contact with our advancing troops, and with them in some cases harvesting machinery to win from waste the crops.

But that, whilst preparing for all possibilities, we were not such optimists as to believe in an Autumn victory, is shown by the fact that arrangements were well in hand to secure suitable training areas for the British troops during the Winter, 1918-1919. For the previous two years, circumstances had not allowed the British Forces adequate opportunities for re-training. But, with the character of the war changing radically, it was thought necessary that they should have opportunities to carry out extensive training programmes in offensive operations of quick movement during the Winter. Adequate manœuvre areas for each Army close behind its Front were sought. It is a coincidence that just after this matter was put in hand military experts on the enemy side were comforting their newspapers with arguments that the new style of Tank attack evolved by the British required very special training of the infantry, and that it could not be expected that any large proportion of the British Army had, or could have, the necessary training.

G.H.Q., when the critical history of the war comes to be written, will surely win high praise for its 1918 work. It took a hard knock in the early Spring and was faced simultaneously with the tasks of holding on, of re-organising a shattered railway system, of training and equipping reinforcements from America and from our own distant Fronts, of preparing for the effective destruction of Pas de Calais, and of organising new lines of supply in case a further retreat was inevitable. From these tasks it had to switch off suddenly to prepare for a great pursuit instead of a great retreat, and did so with such skill and care as the result showed.

How wonderfully, too, the successive blows of the British Army were timed and driven home! As Marshal Foch recognised, it needed supremely good staff work on the part of the British to control that deadly rhythm. Beginning on August 8th, 1918, in four days the British Army cleared the enemy from the Amiens Front. That restored our old lateral line Boulogne-Amiens-Paris and added enormously to our transport strength. We could now hit towards the north, and from the

THE COMING OF VICTORY.

21st to 31st August we fought the last and most happy battle of the Somme, driving the enemy to the east of the river. His position then was attacked concurrently from the north, and by September 3rd he was back on the Hindenburg line, and our Army, flushed with victory and its supply lines working admirably, simply could not be stopped. The bustled enemy did his best to make a stand on the Hindenburg line, and shortened his front so as to allow of a stronger holding there, leaving to us without a battle all of Belgium that he had won in the Spring offensive. But that gave us a new railway advantage, and on September 18th, 1918, the Battle of Epéhy carried the advanced posts of the Hindenburg line.

Quickly the home thrust followed. Between September 27th and October 10th the German centre was shattered and the rest of the campaign on our Front was merely a matter of "mopping up." From August 8th to November 11th the British Army took 188,700 prisoners and 2,840 guns. (The French, American and Belgian armies combined took 196,800 prisoners and 3,775 guns during the same period). When the Armistice was signed on November 11th, the British Army was still full of fight and it had still the means for a further advance, though its horse transport was very weary and the men were having a really hard time in regard to rations and water. But it is safe to say that it was in better plight than any of the other armies. How different November, 1918, from November, 1914! In 1914 so far as the British nation at large was concerned it was a time of desperate shifts and expedients. The lame and the halt and the blind who had fallen out of the Regular ranks in olden days had come back to train recruits for the New Armies. A great new industry of munition-making was being founded. It had to make its machines and its tools before it could make guns and shell. So far as the Army in the Field was concerned it held on against heavy odds and with the scantiest supply of shell to answer the well-supplied German Artillery. Whilst the Germans could send a deluge of shells over we could reply with a bare sprinkle. And we had our cooks and batmen fighting in the trenches whilst the Germans were confidently calculating that the plan of training a new British Army had been irretrievably compromised by the heavy losses which the British Regular Army had suffered, and that a descent on the English coast with a very small force would be sufficient to occupy London and end the war.

G. H. Q. (MONTREUIL-SUR-MER)

There is a legend that the German military plan from the Battle of Mons to the Battle of the Marne in 1914 was prejudiced by the "political" consideration of a desire to crush the British Army out of existence; that to the attack upon the British detachment were devoted forces and energies out of proportion to its military importance. A part, though not an essential part, of this legend is the story of the Kaiser's reference to the "contemptible little army" of Britain. Perhaps the truth or otherwise of this legend will be established when there is a full disclosure of events from the German side. It is not unreasonable in itself, for the presence of the Kaiser with the German Army, and the presence of his sons, without a doubt interfered often with the military dispositions of his generals. In an earlier campaign (that of Napoleon against Russia in 1812) a condition precedent to the ultimate Russian success was that the Czar Alexander should leave his army to its commanders, because he could not act as General-in-Chief himself, and whilst he was with the Army no one else could. The German Kaiser's emotional hatred of the British might well have led to an unbalanced effort against the British Force.

In 1918 it was not the vanguard of a "contemptible little Army" that heard the "cease fire" at Mons. It was an Army 64 Divisions strong, and in all the fighting from August 8th, 1918, to November 11th, 1918, those Divisions had been winning great battles from superior numbers of German Divisions. At the Battle of Amiens we had 16 Divisions to the German's 20 Divisions; at the Battle of Bapaume our 23 Divisions faced 35 German Divisions; at the decisive Battle of Cambrai-St. Quentin our 38 Divisions, with two American Divisions, drove 45 German Divisions out of the Hindenburg line.

November 11th, 1918, saw the culmination of a great military achievement. Of the glory of this achievement the chief share must go to the British soldier, whose cheerful and imperturbable courage and individual intelligence made him a perfect instrument of warfare; but a large share remains for the guiding brain of British generalship in the Field, with its centre at G.H.Q.

THE END.

APPENDIX.

M. Henri Potez, in a farewell article in *Le Journal de Montreuil* (30th March, 1919), paid the following eloquent tribute to G.H.Q.:—

"We know indeed that quite a host of painters, coming from beyond the Channel, have sung the praises of our familiar surroundings, of our clear and happy countryside, of our changing light. Montreuil, little by little, was becoming a kind of English Barbizon.

"Then the War broke out. The presence of the General Headquarters of our Allies made of Montreuil, so to speak, the brain of the British Army. What with telegraphic and telephonic lines, and wireless telegraphy installations, a whole collection of nervous threads radiated from Montreuil, carrying incessantly news and orders. For some months we have been one of the mysterious centres of the great epic. And the silhouette of the Supreme Chief has often been marked on our vast horizons. Our heroes have appreciated the loyalty and the bravery of our Allies on the fields of battle. Side by side the two nations have withstood the most terrible trials in defence of the same ideal. The two great liberal peoples of the West have been the martyrs of Right and of Civilization. At the time of the heavy offensives in Artois, we have seen the splendid troops, who, having set out full of animation and enthusiasm, returned to their camps reduced to mere handfuls of men. These are the memories that can never be forgotten.

"Behind the front, the civilian populations have, on many occasions, praised the affability of our friends, their courtesy and their liberality. War has its exigencies; but it must be recognised that they have shown the best of goodwill to mitigate them. Their kindness on several occasions towards the old people and the children, who had flocked here before the tempest of war, has often been manifested.

"Let us not forget, either, in our farewell compliments, and our wishes for a safe return, those of our Allies who have been represented here by the Missions—Americans, Italians, and Belgians. It is more than desirable, it is necessary, that the great union of the West should outlast the war. It is necessary that the differences and divergencies which may be brought about by the settlement of this crisis should not be allowed to embitter or envenom; but that they should be treated, governed, and regulated with moderation, kindness, and a reciprocal generosity. In that lies the future of humanity.

"'You live at Montreuil,' a University man who was employed as an Officer Interpreter at Lille, recently remarked to me; 'the English speak of it as if it were a kind of magnificent country, a dream city ... they like its peace, its originality, its memories.' Many of those who have lived amongst us propose to pay us a return visit. We shall receive them cordially. We also hope to see again, in closed up ranks, the pacific Army of the olden days, that Army which carried easels as its bucklers, and pencils and brushes as its lances and halberds."

Henri Potez.

MAPS

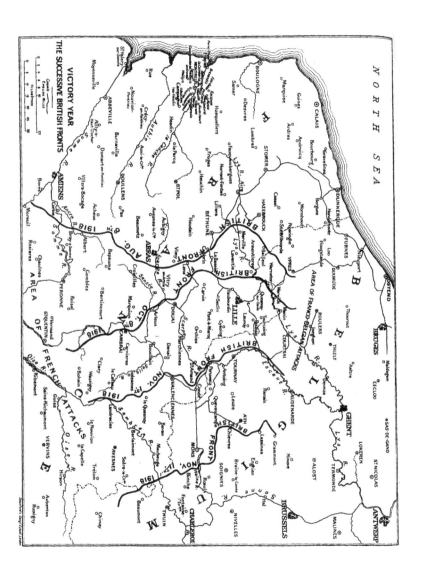

VICTORY YEAR
THE SUCCESSIVE BRITISH FRONTS

223

TO
THE PEOPLE AT HOME
WHOSE UNBENDING RESOLUTION
AND UNGRUDGING GENEROSITY
UPHELD THE SOLDIERS' CONFIDENCE
THIS BOOK IS GRATEFULLY
DEDICATED BY THE
AUTHOR.

QUARTERMASTER-GENERAL'S DEPARTMENT

GENERAL HEADQUARTERS BRITISH ARMIES IN FRANCE

CERTAIN STATISTICS APPERTAINING TO THE PERIOD
8TH AUGUST, 1918, TO 1ST MARCH, 1919

DIRECTORATES AND INSPECTORATES CONTROLLED BY Q.M.G.

Q.M.G.: LT.-GEN. SIR TRAVERS CLARKE

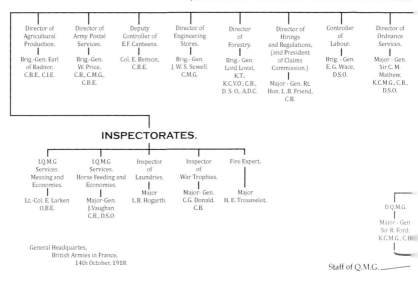

Director of Agricultural Production.
Brig.-Gen. Earl of Radnor, C.B.E., C.I.E.

Director of Army Postal Services.
Brig.-Gen. W. Price, C.B., C.M.G., C.B.E.

Deputy Controller of E.F. Canteens.
Col. E. Benson, C.B.E.

Director of Engineering Stores.
Brig.- Gen. J. W. S. Sewell. C.M.G.

Director of Forestry.
Brig.- Gen. Lord Lovat, K.T., K.C.V.O., C.B., D. S. O., A.D.C.

Director of Hirings and Regulations, (and President of Claims Commission.)
Major - Gen. Rt. Hon. L .B. Friend, C.B.

Controller of Labour.
Brig. - Gen. E. G. Wace, D.S.O.

Director of Ordnance Services.
Major - Gen. Sir C. M. Mathew. K.C.M.G., C.B., D.S.O.

INSPECTORATES.

I.Q.M.G Services. Messing and Economies.
Lt.-Col. E. Larken O.B.E.

I.Q.M.G Services. Horse Feeding and Economies.
Major-Gen. J.Vaughan C.B., D.S.O

Inspector of Laundries.
Major L.B. Hogarth.

Inspector of War Trophies.
Major- Gen. C.G. Donald. C.B.

Fire Expert.
Major H. E. Trousselot.

General Headquartes,
British Armies in France,
14th October, 1918.

D.Q.M.G.
Major - Gen Sir R. Ford. K.C.M.G., C.B

Staff of Q.M.G.

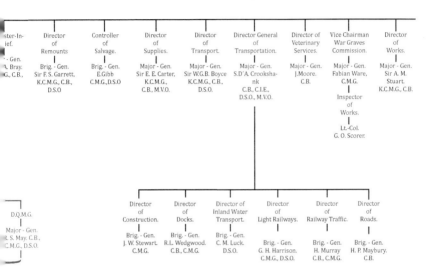

ster-In-ief.	Director of Remounts	Controller of Salvage.	Director of Supplies.	Director of Transport.	Director General of Transportation.	Director of Veterinary Services.	Vice Chairman War Graves Commission.	Director of Works.
- Gen. A. Bray. G., C.B.,	Brig. - Gen. Sir F. S. Garrett, K.C.M.G., C.B., D.S.O	Brig. - Gen. E.Gibb C.M.G.,D.S.O	Major - Gen. Sir E. E. Carter, K.C.M.G., C.B., M.V.O.	Major - Gen. Sir W.G.B. Boyce K.C.M.G., C.B., D.S.O.	Major - Gen. S.D´A. Crooksha-nk C.B., C.I.E., D.S.O., M.V.O.	Major - Gen. J.Moore. C.B.	Major - Gen. Fabian Ware, C.M.G.	Major - Gen. Sir A. M. Stuart. K.C.M.G., C.B.

Inspector
of
Works.

Lt.-Col.
G. O. Scorer.

D.Q.M.G.

Major - Gen.
. S. May. C.B.,
C.M.G., D.S.O.

Director of Construction.	Director of Docks.	Director of Inland Water Transport.	Director of Light Railways.	Director of Railway Traffic.	Director of Roads.
Brig. - Gen. J. W. Stewart. C.M.G.	Brig. - Gen. R.L. Wedgwood. C.B., C.M.G.	Brig. - Gen. C. M. Luck. D.S.O.	Brig. - Gen. G. H. Harrison. C.M.G., D.S.O.	Brig. - Gen. H. Murray C.B., C.M.G.	Brig. - Gen. H. P. Maybury. C.B.

To Major Frank Fox
O.B.E.

As a memento of ... hard worked branch of
the Flags? department - G.H.Q. France - Known
as G.R. - from his sincere friend -

T.C.

228

NOTE BY Q.M.G.

This is not an "official" compilation. Six copies only have been made.

It is interesting because it shews the captures of enemy personnel and important material resulting from our final advance in 1918; it shews also our ammunition expenditure during that period. It is not a complete record of the work of the British forces during that period, since enemy killed, and enemy guns, aeroplanes, transport, etc., destroyed by shell fire or other causes naturally could not be included in the list of captures.

T.C., *L.G.,*
Q.M.G.

General Headquarters.
British Armies in France.
March 31st, 1919.

ENEMY MOTOR TRANSPORT AND AEROPLANES
CAPTURED DURING
PERIOD 8TH AUGUST, 1918 – 1ST MARCH, 1919

Nature	Period 8th August to 11th November	Period 11th November to 1st March		Total
		Ceded by Germans	Found Abandoned	
LORRIES	69	1,275	1,172	2,516
CARS AND AMBULANCES	24	68	936	1,028
TRACTORS	12	30	113	155
AEROPLANES	76	762	47	885

ENEMY GUNS, MACHINE GUNS AND TRENCH MORTARS CAPTURED DURING PERIOD 8TH AUGUST, 1918 — 1ST MARCH, 1919

Nature	Period 8th August to 11th November	Period 11th November to 1st March		Total
		Ceded by Germans	Found Abandoned	
MACHINE GUNS	16,988	6,730	3,697	27,415
TRENCH MORTARS				
Light	1,343	603	362	2,308
Medium	217	24	247	488
Heavy	134	720	57	911
GUNS				
Light	1,602	691	678	2,971
Heavy	417	997	486	1,900

PRISONERS CAPTURED DURING
PERIOD 8TH AUGUST, 1918 – 1ST MARCH, 1919

Phase of Operation	Approximate Date	Armies Engaged	Prisoners	
			Officers	Other Ranks
Amiens	8-2 August	4th	604	19,079
First German Withdrawal	15 Aug. – 30 Sept.	2nd & 5th	48	3,460
Bapaume	21-31 August	3rd & 4th	715	25,483
Arras	26 Aug. – 3 Sept.	1st	261	10,627
Epehy	18-19 Sept.	3rd & 4th	267	8,392
Cambrai-St. Quentin (Phases 1&2)	27-30 Sept.	1st, 3rd & 4th	642	24,850
Ypres	28-29 Sept.	2nd	86	3,658
Cambrai-St. Quentin (Phase 3)	8-10 October	1st, 3rd & 4th	233	10,253
Courtrai	13-31 October	2nd	161	4,436
Second German Withdrawal	13-31 October	1st, 2nd & 5th	123	3,107
Selle River	17-25 October	1st, 3rd & 4th	318	16,200
Valenciennes-Maubeuge-Mons	1-11 November	1st, 3rd & 4th	422	17,643
Third German Withdrawal	8-11 November	2nd & 5th	1	27
Periods other than shown above	-	-	890	36,246
		TOTAL	4.771	183,461
		GRAND TOTAL	188,232	

TOTAL EXPENDITURE OF AMMUNITION
PERIOD 8TH AUGUST - 11TH NOVEMBER, 1918

Nature	Rounds Expended		Tonnage
15-Pdr. H.E.	446	446	4
13-Pdr. R.H.A. H.E. Shrap.	58,405 76,100 }	134,505	1,345

13-Pdr. (9 cwt.) H.E.
               Shrap.
               Incdy.
	294,050
	105,762
	82 }
		399,894	3,999

3-in. (20 cwt.) A.A.   H.E.
                    Shrap.
                    Incdy.
	21,710
	4,912
	210 }
		26,832	383

4-in. Gun. H.E.	12	12	–

18-Pdr. H.E.
      Shrap.
      Chemical
      Smoke
      Incdy.
	6,439,716
	8,500,491
	53,312
	505,506
	14,396 }
		15,513,421	193,918

TOTAL EXPENDITURE OF AMMUNITION
PERIOD 8TH AUGUST - 11TH NOVEMBER, 1918

Nature		Rounds Expended		Tonnage
8-in. Howr.	Mk. VI.	207,305	207,305	20,730
	Mk. VII.	219,827	219,827	23,314
9·2-in. Howr.	Mk. I.	154,170	154,170	22,024
	Mk. II.	194,884	194,884	32,480
9·2-in. Gun.	Mk. III-VII.			
	H.E.	1,164 }	1,241	276
	Shrap.	77		
	Mks. X & XIV.			
	H.E.	1,346 }	1,395	310
	Shrap.	49		
	Mk. XIII.			
	H.E.	9,348 }	9,508	2,113
	Shrap.	160		

TOTAL EXPENDITURE OF AMMUNITION
PERIOD 8TH AUGUST - 11TH NOVEMBER, 1918

Nature	Rounds Expended		Tonnage
4·5-in. Howr. H.E. 　　　　　Chemical 　　　　　Smoke 　　　　　Incdy.	3,769,508 136,946 167,829 362	} 4,074,645	90,548
60-Pdr. H.E. 　　　Shrap. 　　　Chemical	951,547 985,795 13,158	} 1,950,500	6,966
6-in. Howr. (26 cwt) H.E. 　　　　　　　A.P. 　　　　　　　Chemical	3,470,618 53 351,725	} 3,822,396	191,109
6-in. Gun Mk. VII. H.E. 　　　　　　A.P. 　　　　　　Shrap.	152,012 3,454 119,879	} 275,345	17,209

TOTAL EXPENDITURE OF AMMUNITION
PERIOD 8TH AUGUST - 11TH NOVEMBER, 1918

Nature	Rounds Expended		Tonnage
12-in. Howr. Mks. I. & II Mks. III - V	6,983 14,911 }	21,894	7,820
12-in. Gun. H. E. Shrap.	1,127 3 }	1,130	630
14-in. Gun. H.E.	319	319	319
15-in. Howr. H.E.	2,414	2,414	2,011
75 m/m. H.E. Shrap. Gas.	26,453 11,747 2,680 }	40,880	454
3-in. Stokes T.M.	64,190	64,190	428
6-in. Newton T.M.	92,700	92,700	2,853
9-45-in. T.M. Short Long	20 483 }	503	46
	TOTAL TONNAGE EXPENDED		**621, 289**

236

The information on the following pages, although not relating to the period 8th August, 1918, to March 1st, 1919, provides some useful comparisons.

AMMUNITION LOST AND EXPENDED-NOON
20TH MARCH, 1918 TO NOON 10TH APRIL, 1918
(21 DAYS)-COMPARED WITH
HEAVIEST EXPENDITURE PREVIOUSLY RECORDED
DURING 21 DAYS

Nature	Total	Rounds per Gun per day	Previous maximum for 21 days	Rounds per Gun per day
6-Pdr.	94,85	-	-	-
13-Pdr. R.H.A.	211,186	117	-	-
13-Pdr. A.A.	142,636	38	-	-
3-in. (20 cwt.)	15,098	12	-	-
18-Pdr.	5,550,594	89	4,548,019	77
4·5-in. Howr.	1,491,446	76	1,157,457	56
60-Pdr.	651,845	68	369,145	55
6-in. Howr.	1,358,333	66	1,046,955	63
6-in. Gun.	54,755	24	33,761	33
8-in. Howr.	210,604	42	202,545	41
9·2-in. Howr.	162,953	35	166,810	42
9·2-in. Gun.	2,408	7	-	-
12-in. Howr.	8,891	7	13,517	15
12-in. Gun.	167	4	-	-
15-in. Howr.	563	3	1,517	7

DETAILS OF AMMUNITION CONSUMPTION 24 HOURS ENDING NOON 13TH NOVEMBER, 1916 –V.CORPS. 4·12 MILES OF FRONT

Nature	Rounds	Tons
18-Pdr.	133,245	1,665
4·5-in. Gun.	31,640	703
60-Pdr.	5,600 }	261
4·7-in. Gun.	930 }	
6-in. Howr.	13,949	698
6-in. Gun.	200	13
8-in. Howr.	3,604	360
9·2-in. Howr.	7,323	1,046
12-in. Howr.	40	16
15-in. Howr.	70	58
	TOTAL	4,820
= 14 Train Loads.	= per mile of Front	1,170 tons

AMMUNITION EXPENDED AND COST OF SAME AT BATTLE OF MESSINES
WEEK ENDED 10TH JUNE, 1917

Nature	Rounds	Cost
18-Pdr.	1,954,673	£7,818,692
4·5-inc. Howr.	544,782	2,996,301
60-Pdr.	157,976	1,011,146
6-in. Howr.	382,543	2,869,072
6-in. Gun.	11,756	117,560
8-in. Howr.	93,436	1,448,258
9·2-in. Howr	70,972	1,632,356
9·2-in. Gun.	317	7,608
12-in. Howr.	5,480	274,000
12-in. Gun.	153	11,628
15-in. Howr.	565	53,625
		£18,240,246

ND - #0261 - 270225 - C0 - 216/138/15 - PB - 9781910500835 - Gloss Lamination